A YOUNG GIRL READING
Jean-Honoré Fragonard
National Gallery of Art, Washington, D.C.
Gift of Mrs. Mellon Bruce
in memory of her father, Andrew W. Mellon

Maureen Hannan Leroy
Memorial Collection

THE MIND OF THE ORGANIZATION

The Mind of the Organization

On the Relevance of the Decision-Thinking Processes
of the Human Mind to the Decision-Thinking Processes
of Organizations

BEN HEIRS and GORDON PEHRSON

HARPER & ROW, PUBLISHERS

1817

NEW YORK / HAGERSTOWN / SAN FRANCISCO / LONDON

48521

THE MIND OF THE ORGANIZATION. Copyright © 1977 by Ben J. Heirs and Gordon O. Pehrson. All rights reserved. Printed in the United States of America. No part of this book may be used or reproduced in any manner whatsoever without written permission except in the case of brief quotations embodied in critical articles and reviews. For information address Harper & Row, Publishers, Inc., 10 East 53rd Street, New York, N.Y. 10022. Published simultaneously in Canada by Fitzhenry & Whiteside Limited, Toronto.

FIRST EDITION

Designed by Sidney Feinberg

Library of Congress Cataloging in Publication Data

Heirs, Ben J
   The mind of the organization.
   1. Decision-making. I. Pehrson, Gordon O., joint author. II. Title.
HD69.D4H44 1977   658.4′03   76–13326
ISBN 0–06–011818–0

77 78 79 80 10 9 8 7 6 5 4 3 2 1

To Meiko and Frances

Contents

THE REAL CRISIS

Oil resources are not inexhaustible—but that was already known to us years ago. The so-called rich nations have never been so well endowed with scientists, technicians, thinkers, computers, machines, schools and universities, and here they are plunged deep into disarray.

Our territories are blanketed with electric and nuclear power, roads, lorries and cars and now they are threatened with paralysis.

Western countries maintain the most costly armies in the world and now they have become the former rich begging petrodollars from the former poor.

We are told that to govern is to foresee, but our governments are reduced to contending with events that cannot be foreseen.

Is not the real crisis in fact a brain and mind crisis?

Le Monde, October 19, 1974

Increases in productivity will come not only from working harder, but from working "smarter." Only through improved management of our resources—human, natural and financial—will we be able to maintain and improve our quality of life.

From an IBM advertisement

It has become clear to me that our society has become a society of organizations, of which the corporation was only the prototype.

Peter Drucker

Introduction

This is a practical book about a mysterious subject—the decision-thinking processes of the human mind and those of the organization. It is written for those senior executives who are responsible for making the far-reaching decisions which will determine the future strength and success of their organizations. It is also intended for the individuals who must help to create and implement those decisions. What we have to say may also, we hope, prove of interest to students and teachers of organizational decision-making methods, as well as to the general reader who is concerned about how major organizations should carry out their thinking responsibilities before they make those future decisions that will directly influence all of our lives.

In any large organization, the final decision-maker normally has to depend on the thinking abilities of other people to help him reach important decisions. If he is an alert executive, he will recognize his continuous need to understand, stimulate and guide the thought processes of these people to ensure the continued effectiveness of his decisions. However, the methods an executive or a management team should *deliberately* use to structure, develop and motivate decision-oriented thinking processes within an organization is a subject which has thus far received insufficient attention—either in management theory or in practice.

It is, however, a subject of vital importance. We live in an age when major decisions are going to have to be made correctly if mankind is going to survive in a world in which he wants to survive. In today's increasingly complex world, there is a greater need for leaders of government, business and other important organizations to make more correct decisions and to plan more carefully than ever before. The potential social and economic costs of mediocre or wrong decisions—in such situations as those that wrack the British and Italian economies, make international battlegrounds of small countries, bring industrial and financial giants into bankruptcy courts, and threaten thermonuclear holocausts —impose on decision-makers the *responsibility* to understand in greater depth how the thinking efforts of an organization can be structured and guided to produce better and more effective decisions.

The purpose of this book is quite straightforward: it is to try to help the decision-maker to "work smarter" by having him pay greater *respect* and *attention* both to the thought processes of his own mind and to those of his organization. This objective—because of the decision-making factors that are common to all organizations—applies to decision-makers in any organization, from a locally owned business to the largest of the multinationals, from City Hall to Central Government itself—in short, wherever purpose-oriented decisions are taken.

It is important that our focus on *purpose-oriented decisions* be clearly understood from the start. There has been a great deal written about the abilities of man's mind to guide and control his own body, to gain awareness of self, to make scientific discoveries, and to create and appreciate works of art. These are not our subjects. This book deals *only* with those mental powers associated with that sharp edge of human thought which is concerned with individual and organizational decision-making as the desired end result of a problem-solving thinking process.

Men and organizations *both* function through a combination of thought and action. Therefore we believe it is accurate and of practical use to recognize that an organization also possesses a "mind" of its own—that is to say a *collective* mind which includes but transcends the combined individual minds of the executives and employees who work and think together to make an organization function. Before, however, one can attempt to understand how the mind of an organization works, one must first try to understand the fundamental, decision-oriented thought processes of the individual human mind.

Thus, we will argue in this book that (1) the most important decision-making thought processes of an individual mind *can* be identified; and (2) since an organization also has a mind which follows similar thought processes, decision-makers will be better equipped to guide their organizations successfully into the future if <u>they both clearly identify these processes and deliberately encourage the mind of their organization to follow them.</u> We believe point (2) can be achieved by introducing *specific* management systems and practices to improve the thinking efficiency of an organization, and by ensuring that not only "doing" efforts but also *"thinking"* efforts are specifically recognized, encouraged and rewarded.

To explain how the organization's mind can be used to help produce better decisions, we will first present an analysis of the four-stage, decision-oriented thinking process of both the individual's and the organization's mind. We will then discuss some of the barriers to the effective functioning of the organization's mind that exist within most organizations, and how to overcome these barriers. Although these observations will apply to *all* thinking activities within an organization, we will focus primarily on those thinking efforts that are concerned with the essential future-oriented strategic decisions that an organization must make in order to achieve its objectives. And, in order to help decision-makers make practical use of our theoretical arguments, we will conclude Part One of this book with specific recommendations for executive action to improve the thinking efforts of an organization. Furthermore, we will also propose that recognition and use of the concept of the mind of the organization offers managements a new and meaningful framework of reference—and therefore a new, practical tool —which can be directly applied to help them improve the quality of thinking, planning and decision-making in their own organizations.

Many people find that theoretical concepts come alive more readily if they are related to particular cases. In Part Two, therefore, we have included a specific case history of a major management experience that illustrates how the concept of an organization's mind was given practical reality and meaning in the successful accomplishment of a critical U.S. defense program. The management story of the Polaris Missile Program contains the essential elements that relate to the establishment and use by an organization of its unique mind in meeting its decision-thinking responsibilities.

The recommendations we make in this book cannot guarantee success. Most important management decisions are concerned with the future. They must therefore be based on predictions of what the future may hold, and even the most careful predictions can turn out to be inaccurate or inadequate. Such is the human situation. Nevertheless, recognition of the reality of the organization's collective mind and of the possibilities for improving the performance of that mind with the methods and techniques discussed in this book will, we believe, increase the *probability* that the decision-making effort of an organization can be made more effective. Our own experience with senior executives of large business and government organizations has shown that careful attention by management to its thinking responsibilities can produce rewarding results, and that lack of such attention does indeed create serious problems.

To the world of movies and television, the executive of one of the world's biggest businesses is indeed a glamorous character. He's a high-powered operator; telephones ringing, secretaries rushing about. He spouts forth clear-cut, staccato decisions that come from his superb intellect and complete knowledge of the subject. It is, of course, quite different. An important decision is often reached haltingly after the most colorless and heart-searching effort. And, when the decision is made, it is probably with some measure of uncertainty and lingering worry about the choice that has been made. In those agonizing hours, no one could appreciate help more than the individuals who sit in lonely isolation and have no further court of appeal. Any methods would have a warm welcome indeed.

From a speech given a few years ago by Dr. Monroe E. Spaght, then Managing Director of the Royal Dutch/ Shell Group of Companies

Part One

1

The Increasing Importance of Organizational Thinking

We hardly need to be reminded that we live in an era of increasingly rapid change. Supersonic jets, direct-dial intercontinental telephones, telecomputers, tele-Xeroxes, satellite-relayed television, interplanetary spaceships and moon walks are but a few of the innovations that have advanced on us since World War II in a bewildering profusion of movement and information, unprecedented in man's experience. These changes are a result of the increased thinking efforts of man's mind, and of his ability to create and use new knowledge to cope with new and more numerous problems. They are also a result of the sheer volume of available human mental power and of the dramatic increase in demand for that power. This process of rapid change has been further accelerated by the development of massive civilian and military R&D programs, a host of dramatic new scientific advances, increased emphasis on planning, and new data processing systems which use computers as active extensions to man's thinking capability.

Throughout history, however, man has demonstrated that he has been more adept at first allowing problems to develop, and then trying to solve them, than he has been at anticipating them. Now, since the impact of important political, social and economic decisions has become so much greater, the managements of the large organizations which influence or control so much of our lives will need to learn to anticipate more accurately the consequences of their decisions, if serious political and economic breakdowns are to be avoided. And it is *only* with his mind that man can responsibly try to predict and influence the course of the future.

Because today there is an unprecedented range of existing and anticipated problems to be dealt with by organizations, more individual minds than ever before are being challenged and motivated to think about the decisions that have to be made. It is these stimulated and unfettered minds which are creating the changes we are now experiencing—and will continue to experience. It seems obvious therefore that the act of thinking, aided by the wealth of resources provided by modern information systems, will continue to play an increasingly important role in our daily lives.

And yet, given the importance of decision-oriented thinking, it is alarming and indeed puzzling that so little practical effort has gone into trying to understand this fundamental process. Although man has been thinking and making decisions through the ages, he has generally regarded thinking as a natural reflex, like breathing. The mind was a tool to be taken for granted, not one to be interfered with or questioned. Even today, as a contemporary indication of this point, there are hardly any courses in our schools dealing *specifically* with the subject of thinking—what it is and how to improve it.

Our subject is organizational thinking. But one cannot seriously attempt to comment on the critical subject of how organizations might improve their thinking efforts without first understanding the basic thought processes of the original model for thinking—man's individual mind. As Alexander Pope counseled, "the proper study of mankind is man." Therefore, before attempting serious commentary on improving the thinking processes of the organization's mind, we need first to examine the fundamental thought processes of man's mind—to the extent that those processes relate directly to decision-making and purpose-oriented action.

2

The Thinking Function of the Human Mind

In his book *Intuition* Buckminster Fuller observes that:

> . . . until the present moment in history
> Humanity has not differentiated lucidly
> between the meanings of the words
> *Brain* and *mind:*
> They are often used synonymously.
> The pragmatist tends to discard
> The word *mind* as embracing
> What seems to him "untenable mysticism";
> While the realist feels
> That the word *brain*
> is adequate to all his needs.

Fuller then proceeds to identify what he perceives to be the separate functions of what he refers to as the brain and the mind:

> The brain is a special case
> Concept-communicating system
> Very much like a television set.
> It's not just a telegraph wire,
> Not just a telephone,
> It is sensorially conceptual as well.
> It deals with our optical receipt
> As well as with our hearing
> Our smelling
> And our touching.
> In effect we have a telesense station
> Wherein we receive the live news

And make it into a video-taped documentary.
In our brain studio we have made a myriad of such
videoed recordings. . . .
of the once live news,
All of which we hold in retrievable storage. . . .
Now I surmise
That the *speculative thought*
of the human mind
In contradistinction
To the physical experience recalls
of the physical brain . . .
Evolves generalisations
From multiplicities of special-case experiences.*

If Fuller's distinction between the functions of the brain
and the mind is essentially correct, as we believe it to be—at
least as concerns decision-thinking efforts—one can then
identify (1) thinking as an act or process performed by that
part of the mechanism in our heads that Fuller identifies as
the mind; and (2) the complementary act of storage and
retrieval of information, to support the thinking activity of
the mind, as one of the principal functions of what Fuller
refers to as the brain. Thus, within Fuller's framework, we
need both a brain function and a mind function in order to
think.**

* R. Buckminster Fuller, *Intuition*, Garden City, N.Y.: Doubleday,
1973, pp. 117, 120, and 143. (Italics added.)
** Working from Fuller's distinction between brain and mind,
Professor Edward de Bono develops the concept of the "brain storage" function to an important dimension when he observes in a letter to the authors that

I do not believe that the brain works like a computer. I do not
believe that there is a memory part that stores images and information in a *neutral* objective fashion. Nor do I believe that the
thinking mind, like the processor in a computer, takes information
from this memory store and uses it to solve problems. Instead of
this computer model I believe that the mind is a pattern making
and pattern using system. How the mind forms patterns is explained in my book *The Mechanism of Mind*. The mind is exposed
to the environment in terms of direct experience and second-hand

These are the two functions we are concerned with, and we have chosen to refer to them under the headings of brain and mind. Other people may wish to use different headings, but whatever words are used, these two separate cerebral functions need to be identified if one is seriously to consider the subject of thinking. Here, the reader must also remember, in order to avoid any confusion with other capabilities of the mind, that we are not concerned in this book with the other possible and important activities of the mind such as artistic creation, meditation and spiritual pursuits. We are concerned *only* with how the mind works in order to solve problems so that one can make action-oriented decisions.

In the twentieth century we have learned a great deal from the study of neurology, psychology, cybernetics and computers about the brain and about individual and organi-

---

experience through books, reports, etc., according to the sequence of arrival of the information patterns. Once patterns are formed, they dictate the type of new information that can enter the mind. Such patterns are already an organization of information and insofar as one can move from one part of a pattern to another, they are in fact short "thinking segments." We think and then store thinking. We do not store information and then do our thinking. Our habits, clichés, concepts, attitudes are all useful and well-worn patterns—stored as patterns.

The difference between the two concepts is vast. In the first "computer model" we try to find better ways of using the neutral stored information. In the second "pattern model" we have to find ways sometimes of escaping from the stored patterns in order to see things in a different way and that is why I have advocated that we have to develop skill in lateral thinking.

There is no such thing as neutral objective information in the mind. For example, the word "textile" spoken to a group will mean his wife's dress to one executive, a low profit area to another, Japanese competition to a third, labor troubles to a fourth. In each case, the concept of "textiles" is embedded in a personal pattern of experience. Even though it may seem possible to extract an abstract neutral concept of "textiles" this requires deliberate effort and is never really neutral.

For a more complete development of this insight, see de Bono's book *The Mechanism of Mind,* New York: Simon & Schuster, 1969, in particular Section 7. (Underscoring added.)

zational information storage and retrieval systems. But as Fuller points out, man has, as a practical matter, concentrated too much attention on the activities of his brain and not enough on understanding the thinking processes of his mind.

For our purposes, the importance of Fuller's distinction between the functions of the mind and the brain is that it permits one to establish a framework for understanding the thought processes of individual decision-making. With this framework we can then more effectively proceed to identify the *thinking system* the human mind follows in order to arrive at decisions.

Thus, we accept Fuller's *functional* distinction between mind and brain, and we will maintain that this distinction applies to the thinking activity of organizations as well as of individuals. Our first task therefore is to identify and outline the system followed by an individual mind as it proceeds from the <u>need</u> for a decision <u>to the decision itself.</u> In so doing, we will also want to consider why Fuller refers to thinking, at least in part, as "speculative."

3

Individual Decision-Making and the Mind's
Four-Stage Thinking Process

> *What* is discovered by man is never the "universal" or cosmic
> "truth." Rather, the *process* by which the mind brings about a
> "discovery" is itself the "universal."
> Joseph Chilton Pearce, *The Crack in the Cosmic Egg*

When any decision must be taken by an individual, the act of
thinking by his mind appears to us to follow a process of asking and answering a question. Although this apparently
simple observation may not always apply to other processes
of thought, such as artistic or spiritual thinking, we believe
it is *essential* to a proper understanding of the decision-making system that man's mind follows.

There are in our view four clearly definable stages in the
question-and-answer *thought* process of decision-making,
once a problem and/or the need for a decision has been
identified:

1. The Question—Formulating a question to be answered.
2. The Alternatives—Gathering information in order to
   identify and/or create alternative answers to the question.
3. The Consequences—Predicting the consequences of
   acting on each of the alternative answers.
4. The Judgment/Decision—Making a judgment/deci-

sion—by selecting what appears to be the best alternative answer to the question.

The First Stage: The Question

The necessary stimulus to decision-oriented thinking seems to exist either in the form of a question that is asked of the mind (at either the conscious or the subconscious level), or in the form of a problem that is converted into a question by the mind. With this stimulus, man's mind then begins to work through a question-answering process. This observation can be verified by simply trying to think about a decision or problem *without* immediately attempting to answer a Why? What? Where? Who? When? How? type of question. If the answer to the question is already stored in the brain, there is an act of recall rather than one of speculative thought. Thinking becomes speculative or creative only when the answer to a question is not already known by the brain.

Understanding that the mind's decision-oriented thinking system *begins* with the stimulus of a question helps us to recognize the critical importance of correctly defining the initial question to the final outcome of the thinking process —the decision. Conventional wisdom has produced popular adages that illustrate this point, along the lines of "Ask the right question and your problem is already half solved" or "Ask the wrong question and you'll get the wrong answer." Thus, we seem to be already aware of the fact—at least implicitly—that the quality of the whole thinking process and of the resulting actions depend on whether the initial question defines the problem as accurately and completely as possible. Otherwise, our thinking can be led down the wrong road.

Many people find proper formulation or refinement of the initial question posed to be the most difficult stage of the thinking process, and therefore accept the question in the first form in which it is presented. Thus, oversimplified or inexact questions may lead to oversimplified or incorrect answers. If, however, the initial question is carefully examined and is expanded and reformulated as necessary, the mind has already tackled an important and often creative phase of the thinking process. A careful approach to question definition and refinement is essential to the whole effort toward improved decision-making. Without the foundation of a clearly defined question, representing exactly what a given decision applies to and why it is needed, all other steps in the decision-making process can lose their potential effectiveness. The well-formulated question is therefore the focal point that allows and even forces clarity in the later stages of the thinking process.

It has been said that many problems are really poorly defined—or perhaps unrecognized—opportunities. This view is more than a glib assertion of eternal optimists. Time and again problems have produced progress and profit—and again, our conventional language shows it in the adage "Necessity is the mother of invention." And yet, we sometimes fail to see the opportunity presented. Our mind fails to grasp new elements and put them into new patterns so that we see a new road ahead. When this occurs, we may have failed to define the problem or the initial question clearly. Dr. de Bono, in his writing on lateral thinking, describes how thought patterns which have been deeply embedded can and do operate as constraints in sensing the possible dimensions of meaning and the opportunities that exist in any first consideration of a problem. Later, we will discuss how these constraints within organizations can often be overcome.

For the moment, we are concerned precisely with problem definition, an exercise which requires care and discipline in all cases—and often imagination as well. The following four examples from quite diverse fields will help show how re-definition of a problem influenced the final decision or provided the insight which identified an opportunity.

—When garbage and solid waste were considered merely as a problem of disposal of unwanted material, the solutions were limited to that narrow purpose, and the waste was dumped at sea, expensively burned or accumulated in huge, malodorous dumping areas. When the question was rephrased to consider the positive uses of waste material, the potential for clean land—by the creation of new terrain landfills, and the more recent use of waste as recycled material and new sources of valuable energy—began to appear.

—One of the most costly elements in major farming activity is the necessity of moving equipment across the fields in a cultivation sequence. The equipment available in many cases dictates the plant population that can be considered, and each repeated passage of the equipment compacts the soil in undesirable ways. When this was considered as an equipment design problem, the major attention was given to wheel and tire designs. When the problem was redefined in terms of "taking the wheels off the fields," thoughts turned to the use of aircraft for seeding, fertilizing and controlling weeds, insects and plant disease.

—When the problem of vented gas wells in oil fields was considered only in terms of flaring techniques, these vast fields provided spectacular night scenes and completely wasted the gas. When the opportunities for using natural gas as a valuable energy source were seriously examined, a gas pipeline service industry was created.

—When the problem of putting a man on the moon was described in terms of figuring out how a spaceship launched from earth could make a "soft landing" on the moon and then be relaunched from the moon surface for a return trip to the earth, the task was considered to be impossible. When the problem was redefined in terms of how a landing could be made from a spaceship in lunar orbit, the design of the successful lunar module was evolved. The lunar module ("Eagle") that was successfully launched from the command service module ("Columbia") of Apollo 11 while the latter was in lunar orbit landed on the moon's surface with two astronauts, and then rejoined the Columbia and headed for home. In effect, the problem had been redefined in terms of the opportunity for doing something *from* a spaceship that it was known could be put into lunar orbit.

This brief list of examples, which could easily be expanded, gives additional emphasis to this first point that action-oriented thinking does indeed start with the posing of a question as the statement of a problem, and that many first considerations of the nature of the problem are too limited. Expansion of a question to broader dimensions of meaning can often suggest new opportunities, and the subsequent stages of the decision-thinking process can then be made more productive.

The Second Stage: The Alternatives

To be effective for decision-making, thinking must bring order to incomplete and often chaotic information and must then generate a range of possible choices or alternative solutions to the question that has been posed. If the original question is narrowly defined, the possibilities for developing alternatives are limited. For example, "Shall we eat meat or fish tonight?" A more broadly defined question, "What shall we eat tonight?" extends the possibilities for alternative answers. Questions posed in organizational operations are normally far more complex than those which usually develop in personal terms. A simple question such as "Shall we make or buy component X for our product Y?" quickly becomes more complex when rephrased in broader terms such as "With full consideration of the potential for major improvement in product Y through our R&D effort, and our further growth plans that include establishing both component production sources and marketing in country Z, what should our policy be regarding the buying of component X?" Just two additional considerations create more than a simple "make or buy" problem. The opportunities for establishing a welcomed presence in one or more foreign markets become an element for consideration, along with the potential opportunity for eliminating the problem altogether with the success of a radically new design that would make the component obsolete.

If the question posed by the mind is complex, neither the form nor the substance of the answer will become known until the alternatives stage is completed or near completion. Furthermore, frequently work on the alternatives stage leads to a clearer definition or a new definition of the original problem.

Thus, once a question has been asked (perhaps after being refined) and then accepted, the mind's thinking process next moves to the alternatives stage, where it assembles *and* creates the information most relevant to developing alternative answers. This information may be taken from thought patterns already stored in the brain; from new information to be found in books, reports, conversations, interviews, brochures, surveys, computers, etc., and then recorded by the brain; and from various types of pattern associations based on experiences, prejudices and previous thinking efforts, as described earlier by Professor de Bono.

We gather information about the past and present because we need to know where we are before we can make plans to move into the future. But this information is insufficient to enable us to answer a complex question requiring future action. For effective action we need "information" about the *future* as well, and we must create that kind of information in the form of hypotheses, assumptions, forecasts and guesstimates, and not merely rely normally on simple extrapolations from past and present information. The past, present and created *future* information that has been gathered must then be *reassembled* into alternatives which seem best adapted to answering the question. It is during this reassembling effort that a great deal of man's creative thinking takes place as the *interrelationships* of all the assembled information are consciously sought in order to produce alternative answers, or the mind may work subconsciously until a conscious perception of alternatives emerges. (This latter approach is often most effective, because the mind can grapple with complex knowns and unknowns at its own speed, without the confusion that time and work pressures may produce.)

There is a certain amount of mystery about what happens during the alternatives stage. For instance, some writers distinguish between "analytical" and "creative" thinking at this point. In most cases, some degree of each is involved. As a general rule, thinking is *analytical* when a person's mind draws on previous experience or knowledge to break down a problem into its component elements in order to find alternative answers. It is *creative* when the mind produces one or more alternative answers that were not previously recorded by that person's brain. These creative thoughts may be considered trivial or brilliant depending on the question that is being tackled—and the alternative answers that are created—but they are still creative for the individual concerned because they have produced a concept or idea that was previously *not* recorded by the brain of that individual.

The Third Stage: The Prediction of Consequences

With the aid of speculative imagination, intuition and analytical thought, the mind then projects the possible consequences of acting on each alternative that has been identified, in relation to the problem/question that has been formulated in stage one of the mind's thinking process. Depending on the problem and its complexity, these predicted consequences can be, for example, of a moral, social or financial nature. Critical to successful performance in this stage of thinking, in addition to luck or good fortune, are the scope of an individual's knowledge and his imagination, as well as his ability to empathize with the interests and concerns of others who will be affected by the implementation of a particular alternative as a course of action.

This third stage, like the first two stages, can also be creative, because in the process of predicting the consequences of acting on each of the alternatives, new alternatives with a different set of consequences may be discovered, and the need for further new information recognized. This stage is of course also creative because to imagine—whether accurately or not—the future consequences of an alternative does require a creative effort by the mind, unless the prediction is based purely on a previous prediction that has been stored in the brain.

The Fourth Stage: The Judgment/Decision

Once the question has been defined, the alternatives have been developed and the possible consequences of those alternatives have been predicted, then the mind proceeds to rank the most advantageous alternatives for action in order to arrive at a "Yes," "No," "Not yet," "With changes" or "Let's test it" answer or decision. The alternative that appears to answer the original question most satisfactorily is then selected. This is the judgment or decision-making stage in the thought process of the individual mind.

Once the answer has been selected, the four-stage thinking process of the individual human mind is completed until the mind looks for, or is challenged by, another question.

It is relevant to note here that the mind remains throughout the four-stage thinking process in a continual state of asking and answering questions. In other words, once the question posed is defined, the mind then begins to answer such subquestions as "What are the alternative answers to the question?" "What are the consequences of each alternative?" "What is the best alternative?" in terms of the conscious or unconscious objectives of the individual. Thus, the question-answering approach is also applicable to all four stages in decision-oriented thinking.

The four-stage thinking process of man's individual mind can be accomplished in a range of time spans from seconds to years, depending on the difficulty of the question, the time available to answer the question, and the willingness of the individual to spend both time and energy—particularly on the first three stages of the thinking process. This entire process will also normally not follow a neat and orderly, stage-by-stage sequence. The mind can and does move back and forth between these four stages, but in the end it appears to us ultimately to follow this sequential pattern.

The two most important points, we believe, for decision-makers and students of the individual brain and mind to retain from this analysis are (1) that all four stages of the question-answering system of the mind are essential for effective decision-oriented thinking; and (2) that it is a question which starts and maintains that system in motion.

4

The Neglect of the Mind's Thinking Process

Although man's mind is indeed capable of functioning in
the manner we have described, it is often prevented from
operating effectively by the interference of complex emo-
tional forces. These may include such private emotions as
love, anger, envy, self-esteem or fear of rejection, as well as
those emotions fuelled by organizational and hierarchical
pressures such as reward, recognition and status. All of
these forces are closely related to the efficient use of the
mind and must be considered when discussing how the mind
can be disciplined and motivated to follow the four-stage
thought process in either individual or organizational decision-making. In both cases, the more carefully each stage
of the mind's thinking process is approached, the more
probable it is that the final outcome will be sound.

And yet, even those who need most to understand it seem
to spend so little time studying, developing and refining this
process.* People—employees, managers, executives—are

* It is encouraging to note that there are now some practical
methods being applied or developed to help the human mind increase
its ability to think more effectively. For example, we have: Professor
de Bono's work on lateral thinking (Edward de Bono, *Lateral Thinking: Creativity Step by Step,* New York: Harper & Row, 1972) in
which he identifies some *deliberate* mental procedures and techniques for the mind to follow in order to create alternative solutions
to problems; the introduction into the West of meditative techniques
and practices from the East to help "stop the chattering of the mind,"
so that man can think about his problems more clearly and creatively; and the thought-provoking techniques of synectics and brain-

18

not deliberately taught to understand the decision-thinking stages of the mind, nor are they ordinarily rewarded for their ability to think effectively, as such, unless their thinking produces, in due course, an identifiable and acceptable result. In contrast, a great deal has been written and applied concerning motivating the *actions* of executives and employees.

We live in a world where deciding and *doing* are most often rewarded and recognized by organizations, and where decision-oriented thinking is noticed only exceptionally. Even when effective and valued action taken by some individuals is based on the careful thought of others, it is the "doers" who most frequently receive recognition. Although the "doers" *must* receive credit if an organization is to be effective, the reward scales are currently tilted too much in the "doers' " favor, given both the magnitude and complexity of today's problems and the careful thought and planning needed to solve them successfully.

This situation is in part a legacy from a less complicated past when energetically applied simple answers to simply posed questions produced what seemed on the surface to be completely acceptable results. The examples are legion. "Caveat emptor" was sufficient justification for any offering of goods and services to the marketplace. If we needed lumber to build houses, we simply cut down the nearest trees and set up a mill. The consequences of land erosion, ecological imbalances and destruction of a natural resource without replacement were unknown and never contemplated. We now recognize that the earth's resources are finite. Furthermore, faced with satisfying the demands of a human population that grows at an exponential rate, we find it difficult to generate acceptable and effective solutions to the prob-

---

storming can all aid us in generating alternative answers. It is also of interest to note that perhaps by 1980 courses in *thinking* may become common in our educational systems.

lems of such a complex world.

The decisions now being taken by our political, scientific, educational and business leaders are indeed of dramatically increasing importance to all of us. Accordingly, there has never been so great a need for sharpening the problem-solving thought processes of man's mind—*the* most effective tool man has to cope with his present and future problems as he lives through the process of time. His mind must now therefore be used more carefully and deliberately than ever before to develop questions, create alternative answers and predict consequences.

The quality of the decisions taken by the leaders of our most important organizations today depends firstly on the quality of thinking within their organizations, and secondly on their ability to carry out effectively the decisions made. And it must be remembered that these leaders act largely on the results of the thinking capabilities and thinking practices of their organizations. No single person has sufficient thinking power to be able to run General Motors, the Pentagon, or any other large organization entirely on his own. Thus, although it is certainly important to improve the thinking ability of individual minds, it is, we believe, today even *more* vitally important—given the overriding importance of organizations in our lives—to improve the *effectiveness* of an *organization's* thinking efforts—in other words, to improve the effectiveness of the mind of the organization.

5

The Mind of the Organization and the Decision-Thinking Process

The *brain* of any organization can be defined as its information storage and retrieval system, which is fed by the computers, the archives and the memories of the individual brains within the organization. On the other hand, we would define the organization's mind as the collective and collaborative thought processes of the minds of the individuals who think on behalf of the organization. Therefore, at any point in time, the organization's mind consists of all the individual minds that are asked by management either formally or informally, to help provide answers to the Why? What? When? Who? Where? and How?—planning, strategic and operational—questions an organization needs to answer. (We ask the reader to please remember this definition of the organization's mind as we proceed to identify and discuss specific methods for improving its performance.)

Organizations such as governments, corporations and educational systems are formed to serve some collective purpose. To accomplish its objectives, the organization as a whole must perform its thinking and decision-making functions effectively. Although the final judgment/decision stage is crucial, we want to focus on raising the quality of thinking in the first three stages of the thinking process. These initial three stages are as valuable to decision-makers in the fourth and final stage as a seasoned athlete's years of training are

21

to an important match, or as long years of study are to the student's final examination. Thus, if this book is to be of benefit, we believe it will be in helping to increase the organization's ability to bring to the final decision-makers more effective and more thoroughly examined alternatives from which to choose the answers to more carefully defined questions.

As we have noted, one hears and reads a great deal about the decision-making and other responsibilities within an organization, whereas the thinking processes and practices of an organization receive scant attention.

To rectify this situation, we believe that an organization can perform its collective decision-thinking processes more effectively by *deliberately* and *explicitly* following the same four-stage thinking process that is used by the individual's mind. If the decision-making process—or as Peter Drucker has more aptly defined it, "the decision-thinking process"— is seen in terms of an organization's mind, the sequence of that process—as for the individual mind—is as follows:

1. The Question—The development of a *carefully* defined question.
2. The Alternatives—The development of alternative answers by those individual members of the organization whom management considers most skilled at assembling the needed information *and* at creating or formulating the required alternatives or options.
3. The Consequences—The creation and analysis (by the same or different people) of predictions as to the consequences for the organization of acting on each alternative.
4. The Judgment/Decision—The use of judgment by the designated decision-makers to decide which of the alternatives—or which combination of thoughts from the several alternatives presented—should be chosen

to be acted on or tested, or what further thinking effort needs to be made in earlier stages of the decision-thinking process before a final decision can be reached.

In most large organizations, the thinking function at the highest level is in theory assigned to the Board of Directors and the Executive Committee. In practice, however, this echelon of the organization usually serves primarily as decision-makers, as well as also sometimes accepting responsibility for posing the "big questions"—to which the other parts of the organization are expected to respond.

In less complex organizations, the chief executive sometimes assumes most, if not the whole, of the four-stage thinking process as his personal responsibility. In such cases, the organization has a mind not substantially different from that of the individual mind of its highest executive.

In the more effective organizations, the four-stage decision-thinking process operates, at least implicitly, in each of several centers of assigned responsibility and authority. Questions are posed to each of the centers relating to its defined activity. Information flows to the centers to aid these centers in the development of alternatives and in the prediction of possible consequences of action on those alternatives. Each center has the authority to make judgments and decisions. If too many poor decisions are made, people are replaced, but the authority to make decisions is not withdrawn from the center.

In addition, some of the various groups which can belong to an organization's "thinking capability" and which perform in particular the second and third stages of the four-stage thinking process are corporate and operational staff departments, R&D departments, and special project teams that are brought together to think together in order to solve particular problems.

Based on our own experiences and readings, the above

four-stage description of how organizations should proceed with their decision-thinking responsibilities is probably implicitly or vaguely understood by most competent executives. But the subject is far too important to be left to implicit or vague understandings. In our view, it is more *probable* that the quality of key decisions taken by any organization can be improved if the thought processes of the mind of an organization are explicitly identified, understood and incorporated into the routine procedures and practices of the organization.

To do this, however, managements need to recognize clearly that there is indeed a "mind" within their organizations that can and should be stimulated to produce effective thinking. Once they are prepared to do so, they can then also better turn their attention and talents to their other fundamental responsibilities—that is, to defining accurately the major questions to be answered by the mind of the organization; to their judgmental decision-making activities; and to those other executive and leadership roles for which they are held—or should be held—most directly accountable. Furthermore, once the leaders of an organization recognize that their organization does have a "mind," it should then be possible for them to employ more effectively the individual minds retained by the organization by defining, communicating and monitoring *thinking* tasks with greater precision.

6

A Systems Approach to the Problems of
Organized Complexity and the Responsibilities
of an Organization's Mind

Peter Drucker has observed that

> A decision is a judgment. It is a choice between alternatives.
> It is rarely a choice between right and wrong. It is at best a
> choice between "almost right" and "probably wrong"—but
> much more often a choice between two courses of action
> neither of which is provably more nearly right than the
> other. . . . The understanding that underlies the right de-
> cision grows out of the clash and conflict of divergent opinions
> and out of the serious consideration of competing alterna-
> tives.*

The wisdom of Drucker's insight applies directly to the observations we now wish to make.

Most choices between alternatives on which organizations
must take action in the modern world are indeed those between "almost right" and "probably wrong" as stated by
Drucker, because such judgments usually relate to unique
situations. These are situations to which no single "best" or
"true" answer can be found by merely referring to a prior experience or a scientific determination. We can develop this
point most simply by contrast with the great fortune we all

* Peter F. Drucker, *Management: Tasks, Practices, Responsibilities,*
New York: Harper & Row, 1974.

share from living in a universe that does have an order to it. We know that the most interesting and useful facts that man has searched for and found are those that have a chance of coming up again and therefore will serve many times. Suppose, for example, as Henri Poincaré, the French mathematician, reminded us, that instead of a finite number of chemical elements there were billions of them; that there were not some that were common and others that were rare, but they were uniformly distributed so that every time we picked up a new pebble, there would be a great probability of its being formed of some unknown substance. If that were so, all that we know of other pebbles would be worthless. Before each new object we would be as the newborn babe.

Fortunately, this chaotic condition does not exist. There is a great deal of order in our universe. Consider, however, that while man has enormously increased his power over nature through his understanding of the recurring facts and the orderliness of nature, and hopefully will extend his understanding of how to use that power wisely, most major problems that must be dealt with in a modern *human* organization do not have this order. They are like the unknown pebbles in a universe without order. Each problem—and its successful solution—is normally unique to the organization at the time and place of *its* occurrence. It is this *essential uniqueness* of most situations that management faces that limits so strongly the provable "rightness" of any solution acted on. It is also this uniqueness that turns our attention to the best means for developing the "best probable" answers. And the best means available are indeed the human minds in any organization which—by understanding the unique character of particular problems, and by being permitted and encouraged to think together—can be given the opportunity to provide the most useful solutions.

Determining the True Nature of the Problem

It seems relevant here that we not only take note of the essential uniqueness of the problems which organizations most commonly think about and deal with, but that we also recognize the importance of determining the *type* of problem that is being dealt with in order to select the best problem-solving approach to use.

Understanding the true nature of a problem can be helped by reviewing the history of how man has probed for answers. A splendid interpretation of this history is included in an essay on science and complexity in the 1958 *Annual Report of the Rockefeller Foundation* by Dr. Warren Weaver. Dr. Weaver makes the point that *all* problems cannot be thought about in the *same* analytical way. To support this view, he cites the identification of three separate types of problems in the development of the history of scientific thought:

—Problems of simplicity
—Problems of disorganized complexity
—Problems of organized complexity

We believe that the understanding of these three types of problems also applies to the historical development of analytical thinking about the problems of organizations.

Problems of Simplicity

Problems of *simplicity* are those that involve only two factors, directly related to each other in their behavior. That is, there are only two variables. These were the first kind of problems that science learned to attack successfully. When, in 1687, Sir Isaac Newton produced *The Mathematical*

Principles of Natural Philosophy, which has often been referred to as the greatest work in the history of science, he in effect provided a rational framework within which men could begin to search for cause-and-effect relationships in their understanding of natural forces. The seventeenth century through the nineteenth century was a period in which physical scientists learned how to analyze two-variable problems. In fact, they were essentially limited to this type of analysis. During those three hundred years, science developed the experimental and analytical techniques for handling problems in which the behavior of one variable could be described with useful accuracy by taking into account its dependency on a second, and by neglecting the minor influence of other factors. These two-variable problems are relatively simple in structure, and simplicity was a necessary condition for progress at that stage in the development of science.

It turned out, moreover, that vast progress was made in the physical sciences with theories and experiments of this essentially simple character. It was this kind of cause-and-effect science before 1900 which, for example, laid the foundations for our theories of light, sound, heat and electricity. With this basic knowledge of *causal* relationships it was possible subsequently to produce the *effects*—for example, airplanes, television and household appliances— with which we have now surrounded our daily lives.

Problems of Disorganized Complexity

Dr. Weaver notes that it was not until after 1900 that a second method of analyzing problems was developed by the physical sciences. Some imaginative individuals, rather than studying problems which involved two variables, or at most three or four, went to the other extreme and said, "Let us develop analytical methods which can deal with a million or a billion variables." Mathematicians and physical scientists, as a result, developed powerful techniques of probability theory and of statistical mechanics which dealt with what can be called problems of *disorganized complexity*.

An example of this type of problem is one involving balls on a billiard table. The analytical methods of the nineteenth century were well suited for predicting the motion of a *single* ball as it moved about on a table. With considerably more difficulty the motion of two or even three balls could be analyzed. But when the number was further increased, the problems of dealing in specific detail with so many variables turned out to be impossible. However, if the number is increased *sufficiently*, the problem actually becomes easier, as the methods of statistical mechanics are then applicable. One cannot trace the detailed action of one specific ball, but there can be answered with useful precision such questions as "On average, how many balls per second will hit a given stretch of rail?" or "On average, how far does a ball move before it is hit by some other ball?" The word "disorganized" applies to the large billiard table with many balls distributed in a helter-skelter way. In spite of the distribution and the unknown future behavior of all the individual variables, the system of distributed billiard balls as a whole possesses certain orderly and analyzable properties.

A great range of experience comes under the label of disorganized complexity. It applies with useful precision to the experiences of any large telephone company in predicting the average frequency of calls between terminal points and during varying periods of time. It is a method that is also absolutely essential to the actuarial determinations and financial decisions of any insurance company. The motion of atoms and of stars all come under the range of these new techniques. The whole structure of modern physics rests on statistical concepts, as do communication and information theories, which all deal with disorganized complexity.

Problems of Organized Complexity

Finally, Dr. Weaver points out that there are those problems which cannot be solved by either of the first two analytical methods. These problems involve what has been called *organized complexity.* Much of the work in the life sciences in this century has had to deal with this category of problem. For example, "What is a gene, and how does the original genetic constitution of a living organism express itself in the developed characteristics of an adult?" In working on such problems, it was learned that they were neither problems of simplicity nor problems of disorganized complexity. They lay between these two. The number of variables was normally larger than in those that could be analyzed by the first method (concerning two variables) and smaller than the number of disorganized variables that could be analyzed by statistical methods. This third type of problem called for dealing *simultaneously* with a sizable number of factors which were interrelated in an organic whole.

The most difficult problems that man and his organizations face today are problems in this third category of organized complexity, which is why we have given this brief outline of the history of scientific thought as background. There are well-known examples of such problems of organized complexity. We will mention two as a preface to our principal concerns about the kind of organized complexity which is represented by the mind of the organization itself operating internally through interacting human beings, and the kind of organized complexity represented by the external environment in which organizations find the opportunities and problems about which they must think and act.

One of the examples to consider is that of a disturbed human ecology. This problem is one that, in its dimensions, uniquely affects all of mankind, crowded as he is on his spaceship Earth. "Ecology," a word coined only a hundred years ago from Greek words meaning "the study of home," has its broadest meaning for man. Of all creatures, man is the only one who seemingly has been able to place himself aloof from the interactions of living things other than his own kind. He has been able to make a home for himself almost anywhere on earth. Yet, impressive as his accomplishments have been, he has now to realize that he has never left his ecological home. He still needs air to breathe, water to drink and suitable food to eat. He has now found that much of his previous activity is badly fouling his own nest because he did not understand that he was dealing with problems of organized complexity. His assumption—with DDT and mosquitoes, for example—that he was dealing with a simple number of variables was invalid in the prediction of consequences, as residue poisons accumulated in natural life chains until the food that man himself was eating became poisoned.

Other actions based on statistically manipulated measurements of apparently disorganized variables did not give him control of the consequences. Great river dams filled with silt and irrigation systems created sterile salt deserts, because there is an order of interacting interdependency governing the consequences of these acts of which man did not sense the subtle and important nature.

It was clearly a case of "not knowing what he didn't know" that has lead to most of man's present ecological difficulties. There is hope that now that man realizes the depths of his ignorance about problems of organized complexity, he will begin to use the correct problem-solving tools of analysis.

A second example of a familiar problem that can be solved only by first recognizing that it is a problem of *organized complexity* is the problem of the modern city. Here again, the record shows failure to recognize that a city involves a sizable number of factors which are interrelated into an organic whole. Much "expert" treatment of city problems has created more difficulties than it has corrected. The conventional city planner seems to have consistently mistaken cities as problems of simplicity or of disorganized complexity and tried to treat them as such. For instance, many planned cities have essentially represented two-variable planning. The quantity of housing (or of population) and the number of planned jobs were considered to be the two major variables. Action on these simple solutions has produced the horrors of the familiar "company towns" all over the world.

And when probability techniques were added to the analytical tools of the city planner, it became feasible for him to analyze, statistically, various units of the city such as income groups and family sizes. A given number of people to be uprooted by acts of planning, combined with probability statistics on normal housing turnover, permitted an estimate of "housing needs" with statistical accuracy. Thus, there arose the supposed feasibility of large-scale relocation of citizens. In the form of anonymous statistical components, citizens were no longer parts of any unit except the family, and they could be dealt with intellectually like grains of sand or electrons. The accuracy of the numbers became the only measurement of meaning. Nowhere in this approach was there recognition of the complex *organic* whole of a community in which individuals and family units are vital, living, *interacting* units which support and are supported by the richly varied meaning of "community."

As a consequence, in many high-rise, low-income housing projects, the normal supervision of children from the windows of flats, houses or tenements disappeared. The unsupervised street play became street gang activity and a problem to be dealt with only by the police. Small neighborhood businessmen with their adult attention to public law and order disappeared from the street scene. All dealings in problems of maintenance and service became remote and based on completely impersonal telephone contacts. Care to aged and ailing residents became a matter for official social workers rather than neighborly concerns. In some U.S. neighborhoods, children lost the feel of community even in their school affairs as they were bused daily to distant and different schools to support experiments in racial integration.

Thus, as is true of so many parts of our modern society, cities have *interrelated* problems that must be classified as those of organized complexity, and all problems associated with them whether they pertain to housing, transportation, crime, education, etc., or just basic human emotions can only be attempted to be solved through the use of the appropriate thinking approach.

The proper formula for dealing with problems of organized complexity derives directly from the manner in which such problems are handled in a life science inquiry. The approach involves identifying a specific factor and then painstakingly becoming aware of its intricate *relationships* and *interconnections* with other factors. All of this is observed in terms of the behavior (not the mere presence) of other *specific* (not generalized) factors. Two-variable and disorganized-complexity analysis can also be used here, but only in a subsidiary way.

In the modern management language that has developed to describe handling this third category of problem, the analysis required is often referred to as a "systems approach." This phrase first acquired quite precise meaning as descriptive of the approach to the solution of complex technological problems in major weapon and space system designs, where many thousands of interacting components had to work together with micromillimeter tolerances in microseconds of time.

In these, as well as in other, nontechnical applications, the nature of the interacting variables that are to be considered as the elements of the "system" to be finally made functional varies considerably. If the system is to be one of straightforward production (for example, the assembly of automobiles), the well-known assembly line, with its carefully sequenced phases and specialized labor skills, is a good illustration. The engineers who designed a production line of this familiar type used a systems approach simply by considering how all of the many parts—mechanical and human—had to be brought together successfully to achieve a common end.

The analogy of the assembly line has today carried over into the more sophisticated planning of river pollution control. The river is now considered to be like a chemical processing line with many inputs and desired outputs all along the line. Considered in these terms, the control of the river system means identifying and measuring the impact of undesirable inputs, such as human and industrial waste, eroded soils and the chemical runoffs from agricultural land, in various amounts and at various intervals in the system. The varied self-cleansing elements in a river, influenced by dam sites and estuary factors, are all considered. And all along the "line" the input assaults on the river should be gauged in terms of the desired outputs of the river for irrigation, boating, fishing, bathing, human and industrial consumption downstream, with corrective action hopefully being taken to keep the "chemical processing line" in balance for its entire length. Piecemeal attention to particular problems along the flow of a river has failed to provide rivers clean enough to serve even the most vaguely defined purposes.

When a systems approach is used to accomplish some economic purpose, such as the development of an entirely new geographical area, the variables become immensely more complex. They involve not only the planning of complementary business activity such as that of breweries to provide barley feed stock to a livestock industry, but the complete range of government infrastructure development of roads, health facilities, schools and so forth, as well as tax and trade-controlling laws that might be required to support, or at least not damage, the economic objectives being sought.

A systems approach has been applied with great success in the development of an agribusiness complex in southwestern Iran, the Tennessee Valley Authority program in the United States, major tourist development projects, and many other socioeconomic programs in many countries. The term is not merely the latest "buzz word" being used by management. Its simplest definition is found in its own two words. The analyst or decision-maker *approaches* a problem as a *total system* and does not get diverted, because he knows that any solution must be one that recognizes the *interdependent* functioning of *all* of the separate parts, and that he must understand all or as many of these *interrelationships* as he can in order to solve the problem effectively.

At this point, it is useful to compare the history of scientific thought through its three stages and a similar history of the development of organizational operations. Many organizations—whether business or governmental—have long regarded themselves as having only two-variable problems. Many still do. We will show first one of the most obvious and enduring and then one of more subtle influence today.

The most obvious one is simply, "People will work for me if they are hungry enough and I am the only one who can give them a job." The two variables are their hunger and my jobs. This was a solution that worked during the entire early period of the Industrial Revolution. Like the three hundred years of scientific progress using two-variable analysis, there were impressive results from this two-variable management approach. The gains in increased productivity were literally sweated out of exploited, hungry workers, and the gains were saved to help form great accumulations of capital and personal fortunes that could be and were used to create even more productive capital plant and facilities. Dark chapters in human history mark this period in terms of man's inhumanity to man. But we live today as the beneficiaries of that time and may not fairly judge after the fact that a better way might have then been possible. This simple solution to work and remuneration may have been all that was possible in the culture of that time. Needless to say, it is not a solution that works today except in those bleak areas of the world where people still live on the exploitable edge of survival.

Today, two-variable problem solutions continue to have some currency in the thinking of management. One such "sure" solution is the balancing of authority with responsibility in a top position and the interpretation of this balance to mean that, as all *responsibility* for decisions is centered, the *authority* to make all decisions must be equally centered. As a result, the process by which decisions are made can become increasingly self-centered. While there may be a record of short-term successful operations under this mode of management, in the long run it can have a devastating effect on an organization's ability to survive. In this case, an organization, or a department, often suffers the equivalent of a "stroke" when the flow of the decision-thinking process is blocked by the death or departure of an indispensable person who has previously done most of the critical thinking for the organization.

We are concerned with organizations as enduring instruments of society, not as the "hand tools" of particular men, whatever their personal skills or inspired creative brilliance. Most modern organizations must be able to live beyond the influence and without the personal presence of one particularly gifted leader.

Similarly, the second type of problem analysis, where the variables are considered to represent disorganized complexity, has been fundamentally as inadequate in application to an understanding of corporate operations as it has been to understanding the problems of a modern city. The human elements in any organization no longer can be dealt with as mere statistical units, except for the most impersonal purposes. Programs and policies that deal directly with people or staff groups in impersonal statistical terms usually fail to achieve the statistically measured results promised. The reader can quickly find his own examples in the history of a company relocation experience, the pangs of handling a merger, an acquisition or a reorganization, or the introduction of changes in fringe benefit programs or working schedules.

In the following sections we will attempt to give some practical reality to the view that most modern organizations are highly complex living organisms that should be trying to achieve healthy growth and to perform a meaningful function in an environment of change and increasing complexity that continually threatens their ability even to survive. How an organization lives, and particularly how it thinks, is today one of the most important subjects for study. It is a double-barreled problem for analysis. Not only does the organization, as a man-made instrument for creating and coping with change, represent a problem of organized complexity itself, because it has a sizable number of independent human and nonhuman factors which *are* interrelated into an organic whole, but also the environment in which the organization seeks to be effective—the whole of national and often indeed international society—represents a problem of organized complexity. These problems reach mind-boggling proportions when it is further realized that both the instrument and the environment in which an organization operates are continually changing. Yet because the mind of man created both the organizational instrument and the environment in which it exists, there is no reason for considering this dual problem as being insoluble. Man still does have a wondering, concerned and creative mind which he can use to deal with his uncertainties by creating effective alternative solutions to his problems. And the larger the organizations in which an individual finds his place, the greater the number of minds which are available for the effort required to deal with complex uncertainties— *if* the creation and use of the system of this collective mind are given priority, care and attention.

Peter Drucker, in an excellent chapter entitled "The Effective Decision,"* concludes that "the right answer (which usually cannot be found anyway) is not central. Central is understanding of the problem." Such understanding clearly requires awareness of the *type* of problem that is involved in the broadly classified terms we have outlined in order that a selection of the appropriate analytical approach can be made. We repeat that the problems that human organizations face are most commonly those of organized complexity, and the need therefore to recognize that this is the nature of such problems becomes paramount.

In no other area of human thought is it so necessary today to probe searchingly for the possible effects of many alternative and interrelated actions, and through so complex a network of "What if?" contingency questions, as it is in understanding the type of major questions which are posed to the mind of an organization. And this mind can function effectively only, as Drucker counsels, if there is an aggressive stimulation of diverse and dissenting views on what the true nature of a question or problem is, in all of its possible complex dimensions and meanings.

* Ibid.

Perceiving the Mind of the Organization as a System

From our analysis thus far, we conclude that the bringing of the individual mind into mesh with the organization's mind should take place whenever a deliberate output of thinking is necessary. To do so requires instituting a system of procedures for creating effective questions, alternatives and predictions of consequences throughout the whole thinking network of the organization.

In general, however, managements have greatly neglected the organization's mind in comparison with their efforts to improve the organization's brain,* where there have been highly successful developments in such corporate operations as information storage and retrieval systems.

Information, as distinct from new ideas, normally moves rapidly throughout an organization. The impact of a recorded sale on the total response mechanism of a well-operated company is an example of this efficiency: the sale is recorded, billing procedures are initiated, shipping processes are activated, a production adjustment is made, inventories are corrected, the movement in market demand is recorded and its significance is assessed relative to marketing programs. The "automatic nervous system" of the brain of such companies is impressive. There is, of course, also the ability, based on the brain capacity of the modern computer, to develop other automatic systems for calculating, remembering, associating, comparing and communicating information.

We do not question the value of all the developments that have taken place in the organizational equivalent of what we have referred to as the human brain of the organization. But what of the *thinking* processes and *thinking* procedures

* For an excellent analysis of the brain of the organization, see Stafford Beer, *Brain of the Firm,* London: Allen Lane, The Penguin Press, 1972.

which lead to decision-making? Was the problem posed correctly? Were all possible alternatives considered and thoroughly evaluated? Were the consequences of trying to move ahead, but failing, properly considered?

Organizations *and* individuals need *both* a brain and a mind to think effectively. But, to our knowledge, no *systems framework* comparable to that which has been designed for the brain of the organization has been developed for the mind of the organization, to enable and to encourage the individual minds within an organization to think effectively together. Once the concept of an "organization's mind" is accepted, and its potential is recognized, then any worthwhile management team should be able to design an effective corporate "thinking process," just as it is able to institute specific purchasing, personnel, planning and other functional procedures and systems for the organization.

An actual case history describing both the concept and some procedural detail of a management system deliberately designed to create a *decision-thinking organization* is found in Part Two of this book. The history of the extremely successful Polaris Ballistic Missile Program in the United States is included as part of this text because it illustrates in such an encouraging way what can happen when productive and efficient use is deliberately made of the mind of the organization.

Now, our belief that organizations can *deliberately* become more effective thinkers and thus produce better decisions is tenable only if managements are willing to break down their most important functions into "thinking" and "doing" activities (both, of course, often to be performed by the same individuals) and to provide a clearly recognized dividing line between these two functions.

As a general rule the "doing" functions include most of the routine administrative and policy implementation activities of the organization, as well as the information-gathering and information-storing activities of its brain. On the other hand "thinking" activities deal, for example, with planning and the identification of action priorities; contingency planning; new business and product development; problem solving in production, marketing, legal and fiscal areas; predicting future consumer and competitor behavior; and predicting the effect of proposed organizational activity on employees, trade unions, financial institutions, government, the community and the environment.

In each of these areas of *thinking responsibility*, a modern organization would benefit more from deliberately trying to "work smarter" than from merely exhorting its employees to "work harder." Furthermore, most of these areas are also concerned with the hardest problem that faces any organization—that of dealing with the unknown future. One responsibility that cannot, or rather should not, be delegated to any level below the most senior is the responsibility for making judgments about what the future will and should hold, and directing the organization's course toward that future. The future we refer to here is not some vaguely distant time. Its impact is now.

It is the future that dictates the present. This simple truth is a key recognition in developing the mind of an organization as a guiding and creative force.

People act in the present based on their judgment about what the future will hold. They differ only in the span of future time that elicits a judgment and in the nature and scope of present activity that they believe will permit them to live in a defined period of future time. Thus, in this sense, it can be stated that it is management's vision of the *future* which dictates *present* action. We repeat that the time frames for such vision differ in their relevance to current decisions. For example, a mining company considering a multimillion-dollar investment in a potash reserve must cast its consideration of the future in terms of world hunger and agricultural production potential for many future decades and in terms of world geography, both physical and political. On the other hand, a company concerned specifically with serving the Christmas market with suitable products recognizes the short-term demands of that market.

The Planning Responsibility and the Mind of the Organization

Thinking about the future, and proposed responses and contingency responses to assumptions made about that future, are usually referred to as *corporate planning*. This type of planning should be the single greatest stimulus to the systematic development and sustenance of the organization's mind. It is only as a result of well-thought-out plans that decisions can be made more effective and responsive to the dynamics of modern society. In fact, many of the most important decisions—about such problems as resource allocation, action priorities and basic strategies—that managements must make, and the assumptions about the future on which those decisions are based, should be found in their corporate plans.

There appear to be four different ways in which one can think about the future in either personal or organizational terms. These four ways are not completely distinct or separable, but they represent the main approaches.

The first way is the most comfortable. It can simply be assumed that the future will be the past repeated. High-buttoned shoes will remain in fashion; nothing will replace the interurban trolley or the icebox; and the frozen TV dinner is as far as the consumer will go in accepting a substitute for a home-cooked meal. This approach to the future is the least demanding on the executives who take it. They merely have to work on problems of improving the efficiency with which they continue to do familiar things.

Cost-cutting and basic administrative abilities are the only skills they need. The fact that the most efficiently built buggy whip was the last one produced and sold carries no message to such people who have little awareness of the changing markets they serve or the dynamic societies in which they operate. The judgment that the future holds no changes is as much a judgment of the future as the most sophisticated speculative probing of future developments. The fact that it may be a poor judgment does not change that fact.

A second approach is to recognize that <u>there will be change in the future</u> and that there will be many unknowns to deal with. But people believing this can still adopt the attitude that it is impossible to forecast or predict what the changes might be, and that whatever happens, one can handle the problems as they emerge. This attitude toward the future has great historical antecedents. Perhaps the most exciting and splendid chapters in human history were written by men who deliberately sought out the unknown parts of the world, armed with great self-confidence to give force and direction to their efforts. The age of discovery and exploration that dawned in Europe five centuries ago was a time when Western man moved with a very special sense of destiny as he faced the unknown areas of his world, with a bubbling confidence that he could master anything he might discover. Because the world was so uncertain, he seemed to develop an enormous certainty about the part he himself was going to play. During the American Civil War, General Stonewall Jackson successfully conducted his brilliant Shenandoah Valley campaigns with one overriding military principle: "I never take counsel of my fears about what the enemy might do." His confidence in what his own forces could do was fully sustained by the victories that they won as they moved against unknown forces.

This choice of taking only casual note of the impact of future change is dashing and can be most rewarding. It requires, however, that there be a valid basis for confidence in the ability of the organization to successfully meet whatever comes. Unfortunately, the executives who are most prone to hold to this self-confident mood are not normally the type who have the patient perception to probe for a full understanding of just how strong and resilient their organizations really are. The record of organizations that thought they were quite big enough to ride through change, and did not, reads like a Coast Guard annual report on the number of beached whales that had to be disposed of. It is not only whales who are stranded in the shallows with a changing tide over which they have no control and feel no concern. The debris of abandoned cinema houses littered every community for years after television moved visual entertainment onto living room screens, and the motion picture industry awkwardly made its adjustment to a major and long-ignored change.

A third approach to thinking about the future that is a comparatively recent development on the management scene involves dealing with the future through development of organizational plans. Various labels are used to describe this effort. They are called "strategic plans," "long-range plans," "five-year plans," and so on. Often there are also subsidiary plans that find their place in total planning structures under such labels as "operating plans," "marketing plans," "acquisition plans." The literature describing various attempts to blueprint a future crowds the shelves.

Corporate planners enjoy the status and rewards that flow toward their claims of high professional skills in the planning function, and much that is happening in the planning field is very sound. Planning is particularly valuable as it has guided and required executives to spend more time deliberately thinking about the future course of their company or of its specific divisions. Unfortunately, as so often happens with the introduction of new management concepts and tools, the development of plans can have a tendency to become an end in itself. The very conditions which justified the planning effort—the assumptions of a changing world—are often forgotten once a PLAN is bound in handsome covers and assigned for action to various corporate groups. Executives begin to enjoy the false assurance of having "approved a plan" which can sometimes be out of date within a few months. In these cases the organization, with varying degrees of skill, enjoyed the experience of thinking together about its future and conceiving a program for living in that future in a way that was acceptable to the purpose of the organization, but then it turned off its mind and began to apply only its muscle to the actions required to carry out the frozen plan.

The fourth and most sensible approach that can be taken is one which recognizes that an organization can live and grow in a changing future only if it has a deliberately built-in permanent planning capability with the responsibility or mandate to create the changes that it wants to have in its future, or to make skillful adjustments to future changes that may take place through forces outside its control. With this fourth approach, the organization first draws from its past history a clear understanding of its strengths and weaknesses as revealed in its record of success and failure, with careful attention to the reasons for each. It then adds to this awareness of itself studied judgments of its basic organizational resilience to deal with future uncertainties. For example, does it have a strong line of credit in financial markets to accept transient cash flow problems; does it have a reserve of goodwill in the marketplace, and an understanding labor force that will accept and participate in the adjustments to changes as they become necessary; and so on. Such an approach to planning clearly recognizes that while inflexible plans are nothing, a system of planning is everything.

In a word, this fourth approach involves building a planning capablity into the organization that can operate and guide it as an organic entity through its changing environment, *continually* assuring that previously made assumptions about the future are indeed still valid as events and facts unfold, or that adjustments are made when these assumptions are proved to have been in error.

Attention to planning on this fourth course should also include creative consideration of what action would be taken in case of unexpected developments of a major magnitude. As Carl Jung observed, "not everything which happens can be anticipated. The unexpected and the incredible belong in this world." In its broadest illustration, we note the existence of "catastrophe planning" of national governments with reference to response actions on "standby" for natural disasters and for thermonuclear war itself. In the design of American foreign policy, a great deal of planning effort goes into the development of "position papers" covering as many possible important developments as staff can imagine. (The rapid construction of the Berlin Wall by the East German Government was an example of what happened when the United States was caught with its "position papers" down and a great deal of response action had to be improvised.) Contingency planning is, of course, merely an extension of the planning effort of organizations which chart a future course for action under many assumptions of what the future might hold. When the assumptions prove to be invalid, the well-managed organization has a choice of alternative actions to be taken in response to the new situation.

A planning capability requires internal information inputs and participation from virtually all parts of the organization as it moves into a revealed future. In addition, externally generated information inputs are also, of course, resources as importantly drawn into the organization as the personnel, financing, supplies and material with which it performs its organizational function. These inputs to a planning capability can, for example, come from marketing and market research activity that describe actual and potential customers served; information related to competitor and associate behavior represents essential planning inputs; and, with increasing importance, from the inputs that relate to the great range of external social-economic-political changes that can effect a wide spectrum of potential organizational interests.

Such inputs of information must have impact and be given response at the highest organizational levels, where, in the working of the organization's mind in its total planning function, the organization should perceive, will and think about itself as a total being. It is particularly in its contribution to a planning capability that the mind of the organization performs as well as or as poorly as management encourages and permits it to work, by providing the perceptions on which the continual decisions of future organizational direction and action are based.

Thus, one of the key responsibilities of the organization's mind should be to guide the organization successfully into the near, medium and long-term future. The other major thinking demands on the organization's mind concern all of those activities that require short-term solutions to day-to-day problems. Frederick R. Kappel, former Chief Executive of the American Telephone and Telegraph Company, in separating short-term from long-term thinking for an organization, makes a useful distinction between *reflective thinking* and *action thinking*. The importance of this distinction for the organization's mind becomes clear when he observes that

> I use the term "reflective" thinking to cover the mental activity required to ask searching (and sometimes embarrassing) questions about the adequacy of the current operation. This kind of thinking can be disturbing to some men at the center

of successful action, because they may see it as dealing with remote abstractions, with theories of management that seem impractical, and with visionary speculations about the future. The success of a business today, largely based on action thinking, gives the opportunity to build vitality but it doesn't do the building. For that, reflective thinking is essential.

Looking at the business of the Bell System, I know we can reach our immediate goals without a great deal of reflective thinking. But I doubt that we can build vitality for tomorrow without a lot of it, for this is the way we get deeper understanding of our problems. I make this point because I believe the pressures to meet the problems of the day tend to discourage reflective thinking, and when this happens to a business it will surely lose vitality.*

Even, however, with a clear understanding by management of the importance of both the processes of the mind of the organization and of its planning and day-to-day action responsibilities, the organization's mind cannot be *assumed* to be operating efficiently without substantial and continuing management attention to some of the formidable, and in many cases *inherent,* barriers to the thinking function that exist today in most organizations. In the next chapter we will identify and discuss some of these barriers, and then in Chapters 8 and 9 we will make some practical recommendations as to how we believe they can be overcome in order to permit the organization's mind to develop and function more effectively.

* Frederick R. Kappel, *Vitality in a Business Enterprise,* New York: McGraw-Hill, 1960.

Some of the Barriers to the Effective Functioning
of the Organization's Mind

To improve the quality of the organization's collective thinking effort, as we have previously remarked, acts of thinking
must be distinguished more sharply from acts of deciding
and doing. Thinking must precede and must guide action
if it is to be effective. Yet there seems to be a lack of awareness by many executives that the effectiveness of any action—luck apart—is based on the quality of the thinking
which precedes it.

Key executives are most commonly identified as those
persons whose judgment and ability to decide and then carry
out their decisions have been previously associated with
successful results. The ability to choose and implement,
rather than the ability to create, the best available answer to
a question/problem is the most commonly rewarded ability.
Although highly placed executives are often vulnerable to
criticism for bad judgment or for taking action that proves
to be unsuccessful, they are rarely criticized directly and
more fundamentally for failing to create an organizational
thinking system that can produce well-thought-out alternative solutions—and their predicted consequences—for selection and decision.

With the possible exception of R&D activities, certain
staff functions and special project teams, few people within
organizations are recognized, rewarded, or promoted by

management *primarily* for their ability to create or set forth intelligent proposals during *any* of the first three stages of the four-stage, decision-oriented thinking process. The individual brilliance of a particular leader may obscure this organizational deficiency for the period in which that leader's influence is present. But this is sandy ground on which to base the survival of an organization in the present and future world of competition and continuing change. In order to try to ensure survival, the organization must, in its own right, be able to think—as well as act—effectively year after year.

Yet, most organizations today—besides operating in an action-biased environment—actually create substantial barriers to the thinking efforts of their minds. The barriers and the reasons for their existence are readily apparent to any person who has worked in or with large organizations.

Some of the barriers are:

The Personal Risk of Wasted Effort

The alternatives and prediction stages of any serious thinking process *must* involve "wasted" effort by definition. Obviously not all alternatives or predictions of their consequences can be accepted. Ambitious and capable people do not readily want to be associated with apparent wasted effort. If this barrier is to be overcome, the individual component parts of the organization's mind must be persuaded by management that while all proposals and predictions cannot be accepted, their own thinking efforts, if rejected, will honestly not be viewed as having been wasted.

The Personal Risk of Rejected Thinking

Since most of the alternatives presented and the predictions of their consequences must necessarily be rejected in a final decision, the authors of rejected options often risk exposure to ridicule by their peers, and to unfavorable judgment by their superiors—not only for "wasted" effort, but also for "incorrect" thinking. The person who identifies and predicts the possible consequences of a decision is clearly identified with this role if the action taken subsequently fails to produce the predicted results. On the other hand, this same person is rarely applauded for the success of actions based on his earlier thinking. Instead, at this stage, the credit seems to flow most freely to those who take the decision. The fact that the quality *and* quantity of alternatives considered, and the quality *and* quantity of thinking that goes into projecting their consequences, provide the clarity and meaning for decisions that are subsequently taken is often forgotten in the final assessment of a successful result.

Thus, the person who presents a new idea is clearly exposed in most cases. He is most directly and quickly judged on the merits of his idea. If it is poorly presented; if it is thought to endanger anyone administering an existing decision; if it runs up against the often lethal N.I.H.—the "not invented here" factor; or if its presentation is considered to have an ulterior motive, then the "idea man" is an easy target to be shot at by those with the authority to fire. Small wonder that most employees are cautious and seek clues as to what *management* thinks and wants before expressing their thoughts. In some organizations it is a simple rule of survival that one should only present proposals which support or embellish "safe" ideas already well accepted in the decision-making process.

In addition, to avoid "making a mistake" within an organization, prudent and ambitious individuals often try to place themselves in a position where they can limit their thinking responsibilities to analyzing the concepts, views and actions already expressed by others in order to be in a politically safer position and to avoid situations where the possible answers are still unknown. The creative thinker, if he is to survive, quickly realizes the practical realities of these circumstances and either learns to live with his frustrations or seeks a potentially less dangerous atmosphere in which to create and express his ideas.

The Desire for Action

Action does not automatically presume waste, or clearly it would not be taken. Organizations, particularly in the Western world, tend to be action-oriented. The underlying concept seems to be that one will learn by mistakes in time to correct them (or perhaps that the responsible executives will have moved to another organization before the mistakes are identified) and that this approach is considered to be more effective than one of spending a great deal of time, talent and money on considering alternatives, or speculating on the possible consequences of failure. This situation does not appear to be as true in Japanese companies, where they spend, from a Westerner's point of view, an unconscionable amount of time mulling over an important problem before they decide on the solution to be acted on.* (An interesting article by Peter Drucker on this subject appeared in the March/April 1971 issue of the *Harvard Business Review*.)

Most managements generally pride themselves on their ability both to make quick decisions and to carry them out with great efficiency. However, the observation that "what

---

* As this delay is associated with the time taken by the participation of many in the consideration of a proposal, Japanese companies generally more than regain "lost time" in the implementation of the decision once made. The participation of many in a decision-thinking process can resolve in advance many misunderstandings and disagreements which commonly occur in acting on decisions made more unilaterally and then *imposed* on an organization by various authority levels.

is not worth doing, is not worth doing well" should serve as a sharp reminder to those who take these shortcuts, particularly to those who have helped to build the mystique that the mere act of deciding has an independent value, without regard to the quality of the decision taken.

Of course, excessive concern with uncertainties can result in undesirable inaction. We want only to suggest that it is perhaps time to strike a *new balance* in many management value systems, and particularly to curb the excessive influence of those high-riding "doers" who have for too long been able to dismiss orderly and thoughtful attention to the alternatives and consequences in their impatience to "do something."

The Dislike of Uncertainty

Thinking hard about important problems of the organization with no known or certain answers is *not* easy for most people. Analyzing known and proven information is much more comfortable. As a result, individual minds trying to work through the ambiguous alternative and consequential stages of thinking are often called "muddled," and the persons so occupied are frequently referred to as "indecisive," "daydreamers" or worse. People who prefer to end the *work* of exhaustive thought by making quick decisions instead of continuing to generate and ponder other possible alternatives and their consequences are often considered to be "decisive" and, oddly enough, "clear thinkers." Unless creative thinking individuals in an organization can be persuaded that management understands the inherent problems of uncertainty involved in organizational thinking efforts, the mind of the organization will probably produce stale, stereotyped versions of comfortable, conventional wisdom.

The Need for the Infallibility of the Boss

As a practical fact of organizational life, an executive, to establish and maintain his authority, *must* perceive his role as being that of judge, decider and leader. Thus, in order to maintain the confidence of his colleagues and his subordinates, he cannot and *should not* normally be seen by his subordinates to be too *directly* connected with the creation of any "losing" thought that could ultimately be rejected— whether it be an alternative or a predicted consequence. This is one very fundamental and practical reason why many of the thinking functions of the mind of the organization *must* be delegated and why effective leaders who wish to continue to be effective must encourage that mind to flourish.

The Stifling Influence of the Personality of the Boss

Often there are also restrictions placed on the functioning of an organization's mind by the personality of the chief executive. The problem of personality takes many forms and can range from the leader who simply believes that he is the only one capable of generating alternatives, predicting consequences and making decisions, to the person who feels that his working and thinking habits are "best" and therefore must be followed by others. There are many forms in which such an impeding influence finds expression. The chief executive may associate a tidy (or untidy) desk with productive effort, have a color preference for office decor that he feels should become standard, believe that all people think best at the same hours of the day or in other ways impose his own concept of the "most productive environment" on all of his subordinates.

The Deadening Effects of Bureaucratic Controls

The imposition of the personal predilections of a boss fails to recognize that the *thinking* activity and approach of each individual is a highly personal affair, subject to individual preferences and habits. Equally as serious as such personal matters is the often deadening effect of unimaginative and impersonal controls and routines. Frequently one finds in organizations that "whiz kids" whose first years are crowned with brilliant success gradually become slaves to routine administrative schedules and patterns. This can be due merely to the aging of the individual, but more commonly it results from the overly rigid controls that an organization applies in the name of supervisory review and analysis. Such controls can and do suffocate individual brilliance of thought. Controls elaborately designed to prevent small errors too often delay or deny major successes. Furthermore, they stifle the free play of what should be unfettered minds endeavoring to do what the organization should want them to do—*think*.

The "bureaucratic controls" barrier to effective thinking seems to be common to all organizations, large and small, with few exceptions. It currently has become more evident in the increasing regulation of the U.S. and other national economies, and the proliferation of "categorical grants in aid" for health, education and welfare purposes by a "big government" bureaucracy. (The proponents in the United States of what is now called "the new federalism" wish to permit more local government and community thinking and decision-making on the priorities of local needs and are seeking to reverse the trend of the past four decades toward increasing the often deadening influence of central government authority.)

Another example that relates to this particular barrier to

the mind of the organization occurred during the post-Korean War period in the Department of the Army. It involved a major reorganization of the logistic support command of that Department. A consultant was asked to review a six-foot pile of regulations, and the reporting required thereunder, concerning the operation of the Army's vast field establishment of production, maintenance and supply installations. The consultant was asked to make recommendations for eliminating those regulations which were out of date and unnecessary. After studying the matter, his conclusions were devastating. He said,

> Your entire management approach is wrong. You have created this mountain of regulations on the basis of four assumptions. Each and every one of the four is wrong. And if they were right, your fifth and most important assumption about the way you are running your field establishment would be wrong.

In explanation of this analysis he made his points as follows:

> *First* you have assumed that there is indeed a single best way to do everything that is required at your field stations. The range of things on which you have acted under this assumption is completely incredible and covers everything from how to operate a tank repair shop to how to nail boxes and kill rats. This first assumption is wrong. There is no single best way to do each of those things.
>
> Your *second* assumption is that you have people at head office smart enough to find out what this best single way is for each of the subjects covered. This assumption is wrong. There are probably not any such best solutions and if there were you couldn't possibly organize the resources capable of finding out what they are from assignment to a Washington office.
>
> Your *third* assumption is that these "best solutions," once found, can be described in the stilted language of Army regulations that will be understood by all of the people you are holding accountable for compliance. This assumption is also

wrong. Your basic communication system is primarily designed for "Command" messages and not for management information or advisory circuits.

Your *fourth* assumption is that your field installation commanders will blindly comply with all the trivial detail in this library of regulations, and that compliance can be audited by a large body of field inspectors. This assumption is wrong. Unfortunately, some will probably try to make all of their decisions "by the book" but the Army has enough mature executives so that there will be some who will say "To hell with the book, I'm going to do this job the way I know it should be done at my station."

Now, even if all of the above four assumptions proved to be valid, then your *fifth* assumption, the most important of all, would prove to be wrong. You assume in all of your efforts that you are managing your field plants and stations in a way that would make them completely responsive to the demands of the Army at war. If you run these operations with men who are no more than robots who have to look up all their answers in a book, they cannot be expected to respond to any of the demands on them "when the balloon goes up," and the character and tempo of their activity undergoes great change. You will probably have to re-staff much of your establishment to make it capable of flexible, imaginative and responsive support to the war needs of your Army.

The consultant then went on to recommend the preparation of a new concept of command-management relationships that was based on performance rather than on simple compliance with regulations. Meaningful recognitions were to be given for the continual flow of new ideas and experiences that had proved to be locally successful, and which might prove adaptable by choice, not by order, to other situations.

There is no particularly "happy ending" to this story. When the Army support system was indeed again placed under war stress, the management response was to make another major reorganization move. It is not known what happened to that six-foot pile of regulations.

Most retail network operations also suffer in varying degrees from the influence of remote staff groups who use the authority of central office positions to impose their concepts of "standardized methods" on widely different field situations, which need the freedom to innovate and make local market adaptations. The stifling influence of hierarchy and bureaucratic controls on the thinking processes of such organizations has sent many into bankruptcy.

Day-to-Day Pressures

Most people in an organization who are potentially capable of making valuable contributions to the effective functioning of the organization's mind are under such day-to-day pressures to put out grass fires and keep the administrative routines going—particularly in our present age of rapid change—that they lack the *indispensable* time normally required to perform the more complete reflective thinking function to which Mr. Kappel refers. Instead of being able to ask even the continuing question, "Why do we do things this way?" much less the larger strategic questions, "Where should we be going?" and "What does the future have in store for us?" they are continually reacting to the problems of the present. They are, in fact, as the American archeologist Loren Eiseley has put it, "pursuing the mind-destroying drug of constant action."* "I am dominated by my in-basket" is a common complaint of the overpressured executive and his staff. Yet, the present is changing with increasing speed, and the responsibility for reacting to change becomes ever more demanding of careful thought.

* Loren Eiseley, *The Unexpected Universe,* London: Gollancz, 1964, p. 6.

Thus, those individuals within an organization who wish to be effective must be ruthless in allotting their time, energy, and thinking capabilities to only those subjects that really matter.

The Organization Box Mentality

In 1665 Robert Hooke first looked through his newly invented compound microscope at a sliver of cork and saw that it was built of extremely tiny compartments. He decided to call these compartments "cells" because they reminded him of the rooms in a monastery. He drew the pattern of these cells and passed them around to his associates as interesting examples of what could be revealed under a microscope. In following years, similar patterns of the cell structure of other tissue were drawn and marveled at. It was not until almost two hundred years later, in 1860, that a German pathologist, Rudolf Virchow, first asserted that every living organism, even the largest, began life as a single cell. Five years later, the Austrian botanist and biologist Gregor Mendel demonstrated the laws of heredity. His work, together with other studies, suggested that the secrets of life itself are in the core of the living cell. Now, cell theory is to biology approximately what atomic theory is to chemistry and physics.

This observation is more than a distracting comment. It gives us a reference for the unhappy judgment that a "dead cell" awareness of corporations is still very much with us. We recognize it in the fascination with the patterns of an "organization chart." The original resemblance to a monastic cubicle that gave the cell a name, with all of its cloistered significance, remains in the meaning of many organization charts. An excessive concern by executives for the *literal* meaning of organizational charts, with their series of neat rectangular boxes in pyramidal patterns of relative authority status, is an important barrier to effective organizational thinking. Such charts do show "line of command" relationships, but they fail completely to bring out the truly *interdependent* nature of all corporate activity. Indeed, they often encourage the occupants of each such designated box, like so many birds in a forest exercising territorial claims, to develop their own protective measures to maintain isolation from the world outside their own "patch." Organizational boundary disputes form the basis for a great deal of the internecine warfare that goes on in organizations, and are indeed formidable barriers to the effective performance of the organization's mind.

An uneasy truce is often reached between the executives or managers occupying the various boxes based simply on mutual agreements that "if you stay out of my box, I'll stay out of yours," but, once this happens, the damage to the organization's mind has been done.

In such companies the living, interacting relationships of support and dependency that tie all corporate parts or "cells" into an organic whole are not even recognized as the variables in solving a complex problem. The cells are rarely regarded as the sources of creating ideas, or of adaptation to a changing environment in which the organization may have to change form or function. When one looks inside the dry and isolated cells of such companies, one finds what seem more like moribund pupae than people, each person tightly wrapped in the cocoon of a restrictive job description. It is small wonder that there are few signs of creative life in companies where the organization chart and the file of job descriptions represent the principal effort that has been made to describe how the company lives.

This is not merely a petulant protest against attention to organizational anatomy and to the definition of work tasks. There has certainly been a necessity for attention to properly placed organizational parts, even though some organizations seem to be engaged in a constant reshuffling of their parts, and the wry comment of the employee who said "If my boss calls, find out who he is" is more than a cartoon line. It is just that the anatomical approach to management studies so often seems to represent very little advance on the insights of the most ancient men, who knew of the existence and place of the larger organs such as the liver, heart, lungs, stomach and so forth, but who had no knowledge of the separate and interacting functions of these organs. The word "anatomy," coming from the Greek, means "to cut up," and that is what many organizational experts do in their approach to management studies. They are principally concerned with cutting up the body to see if the organs of a corporation are in the "right" places. Where the emphasis is on place rather than purpose, it is no great surprise if a company dies or goes into deep shock from the relocation of its parts as things are "put in order."

Study of organizations has, of course, progressed beyond crude anatomy into at least partial understanding of corporate "physiology" and a concern with function. Most of this attention, however, has been directed to the functioning of the *separate* parts. The management literature fills the shelves and crowds the agenda of conferences and seminars with titles dealing with such functions as "Sales," "Production," "Purchasing," "Finance," "Public Relations" and all of the other separate functions that a corporate body performs in its efforts to stay alive and to grow as a total organism. There has been brilliant work done in improving the functioning of individual corporate parts.

Here we are concerned, however, with the ability of the organization to think as a *total* entity, and its ability to adapt to a changing world as a *total* entity. And one of the specific actions that can be taken to achieve these abilities is that of breaking down the barriers that have grown up from the mystique of the organization box. The reality of modern organizational life requires that each center of established authority recognize that it has responsibilities in each of three areas, two of which exist outside of its own direct authority. For the sake of simplicity, these can be defined as areas of "direct," "supporting," and "monitoring" responsibility. An example illustrates: The purchasing officer has direct authority that applies to the function of purchasing. However, this officer should also accept responsibility for *supporting*, with properly scheduled product delivery, every existing and proposed new marketing program. He should be completely knowledgeable about and participate in the design and scheduling of those marketing programs which involve a purchasing service. This same officer has the further responsibility for *monitoring* or keeping himself informed of progress on other corporate decisions, such as one to build a new plant or one to change product supply from a "buy" to a "make" source. He needs to monitor this progress in order to plan his own purchasing activity. Similar examples exist in all functionally separated organizational parts.

When rigid, self-protective "organization box mentalities" exist in a company, it is not possible for information or ideas to flow across these barriers. All problems and opportunities are defined in narrow functional terms, and it becomes virtually impossible to stimulate *responsible* thinking that reaches beyond the limits of the functional boundaries reflected in the organization charts.

A Rigid Accountability System

An unfortunate corollary of the "organization box mentality" barrier to effective thinking and problem solving is found in the rigidity of financial accountability systems that provide performance measurements for various defined and organized functional groupings.

When executives know that they are being evaluated on the basis of a narrowly defined functional performance, there is little incentive to participate in problem solving which, although it might be advantageous for the organization as a whole, would have a negative effect on the measured performance of their special functions. Again, an example illustrates: If the problem is one of optimizing an inventory position to the greatest advantage of a company, there is a built-in potential conflict among at least three important parts of many organizations: finance, marketing and production.

Having the lowest possible inventories supports the cash flow and financing interests of the Finance Officer. Financing inventories is often difficult and always expensive. The Marketing Officer, however, will wish to maximize inventory positions in order to best serve his customers. The Production Officer will wish to establish inventory levels that permit the most efficient use of production facilities and thereby minimize his production costs.

However, given an accountability system that provides separate performance results for each of these three parts of the organization, either the typical inventory problem goes unresolved or a fourth "staff" element is created to establish and impose the optimum solution on all other parts of the organization which could not think effectively together.

*   *   *   *   *

All of the above are real and common barriers to the effective functioning of the organization's mind. The decision to overcome effectively these barriers represents a considerable challenge to any responsible management team.

8

Dismantling the Barriers—A Question
of Management Attitude

There are no quick or easy methods for overcoming most
of the organizational barriers to the effective functioning of
the organization's mind to which we have drawn attention.
However, once management adopts a positive attitude toward the thinking function and thinking responsibility of its
organization, then there are indeed specific practices which
can be introduced to improve the performance of the organization's mind. Some of these we discuss in this and the
next chapter.

Before instituting these new practices, however, management must first of all adopt the right attitude toward the
mind of the organization. The working environment for the
organization's mind *can* be improved, but to do so, management must be willing to go to sufficient trouble in order *deliberately* to understand, create and maintain both the positive conditions and the operational systems which will allow
individual minds to work together effectively. One principal
requirement, therefore, for the effective operation of an
organizational mind is a clear understanding of the thinking
process of management itself in its rational pattern of asking
and answering questions.

The Thinking Process of Management

The process of management—or what we would call the thinking process of management—has been described in many ways. There is probably no single subject that has been so analyzed in fragmented pieces since the legendary seven blind wise men tried to describe an elephant after feeling various separate parts of the animal.

Some have written of this subject in ponderous prose, dealing with it in terms of the structure of authority—with all thought and action dictated by the exercise of and response to "power." *Power-oriented* organizations make very effective armored tank divisions. But it is the *problem-oriented* organizations which deal most effectively with the fluid, changing facts of life in a modern society where response requires more than compliance to the simple command "Charge!"

Others have approached the subject and then given up, settling for simple definitions like "The meaning of management is found in the word itself, that is, management means 'man' leading 'men' through a period of time."

We have found little practical use in such efforts to *define* a subject whose useful *understanding* is so important to all members of any organization. We believe there is in fact a unified concept of the process of management which applies to the action-oriented purposes of any person or organization. The thinking, deciding and acting process depicted in Exhibit A actually is as relevant for a thoughtful consumer's shopping trip as for the deliberations of a large multinational corporation.

The entire management process involves asking a set of questions and then deciding to act on the answers which seem to have the most desired consequences. These questions are the familiar six:

EXHIBIT A

THE MANAGEMENT PROCESS BY FUNCTIONS

BASIC CREATIVITY

POLICY-MAKING

APPLIED CREATIVITY

ANALYSIS

PRELIMINARY MEASUREMENT

OPERATIONS

FINAL MEASUREMENT

BASIC REVIEW

DECISION POINT

"Go Ahead" . . . "Revise" or "Drop"

DECISION POINT

"Go Ahead" . . . "Revise" or "Drop"

DECISION POINT

"Go Ahead" . . . or "Drop"

FINAL COMMITMENT POINT

"Go Ahead" — or "Drop"

PRELIMINARY DECISION POINT

"Worth Looking Into" — or "Forget It"

Development of "Best Approach"
Determination of Alternatives, Their Pros and Cons — and Selection of the Right One

Establishment of Objectives and Policies
On Basis of the Facts . . . What to Aim for — Long Term and Step by Step

Development of Specific Action Plans
Details of Actions, Personnel Facilities, Schedules, Costs, and Coordination

Integration and Analysis of FACTS
Determination of Adequacy and Validity of Facts . . . and What They Indicate

Implementation of the Program

Finding and Assembling of FACTS
Total Market — Trends — Competition Investment — Volume and Profit Potential

Measurement and Reporting of Progress
Determination of Criteria of Progress, and Actual Reporting

What Needs to be Done

EVALUATION

What Has Been Done

—Why do we want to do something?
(What are our objectives?)
—What should we do to achieve our objectives?
(What action should we take?)
—When should we act?
—Where should we act?
—Who should be involved in our action?
—How should we proceed?

The reader will note that this sequence of six basic questions and answers in the management thinking process is usually *cyclical* and not linear. It is cyclical because after most actions taken there is a need to measure and evaluate the success or failure of the action taken and this information becomes a feedback input to the entire process as future action is considered.

The concept of the cyclical management process as shown graphically in Exhibit A is, we believe, understandable as drawn, but it is important to note the following:

1. The purpose of the exhibit is to emphasize that there are question-raising and question-answering functions throughout the entire management process.
2. The process, as with planning, is normally a continuous one. It is not one that starts, stops and then starts again.
3. There are four major decision points which must be passed through before the final commitment for action is made.
4. Once the management thinking process begins functioning in this cyclical pattern, there is a thinking activity involved at all points in the cycle, for different subjects, at all times.

To study the chart, one should begin with the place marked "Evaluation," where attention is given first to the question, "What needs to be done?" In evaluating what needs to be done, the organization looks not only to what it has been doing, but most important, it looks outside of itself and tries to perceive with imagination present and future problems and opportunities which are relevant to its own operations and objectives. This place in the management cycle has sometimes been likened to a military "radar scanning or tracking station" for the receipt of signals. The analogy can usefully be expanded to suggest that this is the place for a battery of "radar stations," each one to cover a different sector, such as competitor behavior, consumer habits, new technology, new ideas, government and community moods and influences, the state of the economy and other more specific areas of interest.

The following three examples illustrate the receipt of and reaction to some of the intelligence messages that might flow into an organization at this point:

1. The pollution problems and lawsuits that followed from the disposal of the poisonous chemical Kepone in the James River of Virginia by a chemical company might well stimulate other chemical companies to consider tightening their own control and disposal procedures and to ask, "Should we obtain an outside technical audit of our own operations to ensure that we have exercised due diligence in our social and legal responsibilities on this type of matter?" The same event, however, would be of little interest to a company marketing a line of jewelry.

2. Many parents use their television sets to entertain and educate their children, because they have neither the time nor perhaps the interest to personally instruct them. There is also evidence of growing market for the use of "audio books." A publisher of children's

books might well decide to take a detailed reading on these two observations and ask, "Is there a potential growing market for audio books as a substitute for bedtime storytelling?" If there were a "Yes" answer, the first "preliminary decision point" would be passed, and the finding, assembling and analysis of the most relevant data would begin. This same message picked up on the "radar scope" of a company engaged in the production of heavy earth-moving equipment would of course not enter the management process of that company at all.

3. A change in airline rates by a government regulatory body which expanded the opportunity for offering more attractive "packaged holidays" would be of great interest to the management of companies in the travel business, and the message would have an immediate impact on the management process of such companies. The change in a regulation would not be especially relevant for most other companies, except as a possible fact to be considered by an alert personnel director for an employee incentive program.

The function of the "radar station" can be handled in many various ways. Some organizations have established their own formal or informal "think tank" operations to scan present and future environments. Others subscribe to special study efforts by professional groups to assess developments in specific areas of interest such as "the future of the privately owned automobile in modern societies." Some simply encourage extensive subscription to periodicals relating to matters of corporate interest in the hope that somewhere in those great piles of paper, someone will find a few points of possible interest to the organization. Then there are other companies that do not even bother to "look out the window" at what may be going on outside, but concentrate merely on what they can learn from their narrow fields of operation.

Whatever the form of exposure to external developments, some messages will pass through the first preliminary decision point in the management process and stimulate the first sets of questions, designed to permit the "preliminary measurement" and then the "analysis" of data, and to set the stage for the next decision point. At this stage, the facts and their measured significance are judged for their impact on existing organizational objectives and policy. It is here that the "Why" and the "How" or the policy questions need to be answered. If, for example, an opportunity being analyzed involves acquiring a new outlet in a new part of the country or the world, and the company does have an objective of expansion into this new territory, then one "objective" test of "Why" has been met. If, however, the particular acquisition is available only through a joint venture, and the company *policy* is to expand only through complete ownership control of its operations, then the subject would not move through the next decision point. If the opportunity is a completely new one, such as a diversification move, and the organization had neither objectives nor policy to cover the situation, then the questions would relate to the possible shaping of new objectives and policy.

If the "Why" question and the big "How" question of policy have been satisfactorily answered, a third decision is required to determine "What is the best action that should be taken to support the proposal?"

At this point, the most serious range of alternatives for action should be examined. If, for example, the decision involves introducing a new product, the questions selected will determine the detailed answers to *where* to set up the test market, *when* to schedule the test, *how* to develop the test market through promotion and customer sampling, and *who* to involve in the efforts. These specific action plans are the basis for approaching a Final Action Commitment Point. If the decision for commitment is made, the proposal is implemented in the phase noted as "Operations."

The management process now moves through the measurement function, as attention is given to the results of the operations, and information flows back to the "Evaluation" stage both to support judgments of "What has been done" and to combine these judgments with consideration of "What now needs to be done," which was the starting point in this brief description of the continuing management process. Again, it is at this point that input messages from the "outside world" and internally generated information are used to provide a new point of departure for the entire process.

There has been a great deal of attention given to many specific phases in this cyclic process:

1. Accounting systems, information and performance reporting systems, as well as internal auditing procedures and other measurement and reporting techniques, have been developed dealing with the question "What has been done?"

2. There have been excellent innovations developed for dealing with the scheduling questions which require When answers.

3. Many sophisticated measurement techniques exist for developing answers to the Where questions in terms of site selections and definitions of "market-served areas."

4. There is much guidance available for dealing with the Who questions in the literature dealing with organizational principles and the selection of human resources.

5. Procedures, instruction manuals and handbooks abound covering a complete range of <u>How</u> questions and answers.
6. And there is a growing amount of attention given to the planning function, which addresses the <u>Why</u> question in varying ranges of future time.

Our main purpose here, however, is to give some practical reality and meaning to the *total* management process, and to highlight the fact that executives who understand the cyclic sequence of the process need deliberately to develop the thinking capabilities of their human resources in order to prepare for the entire series of questions and decisions required to *sustain* the process. The exhibit we have drawn could usefully be subtitled "The Life Cycle of an Idea Within an Organization" to place an even clearer focus on how the individual elements of an organizational mind are *needed* to move ideas and proposals forward to action decisions. In fact, *each* idea that is considered for action by the organization would or should pass through this cycle.

As noted earlier, the decision-thinking process is applicable to all decision-oriented thought, from personal levels to the largest organizations. Even a consumer's reaction to news of a possible sugar shortage can be traced through the phases outlined in the exhibit. She might pass through them rather quickly before heading for the supermarket, but she would have touched base with each step along the way. In Part Two, which deals with the management of the Polaris Missile Program, we note an example of a very large national effort that involved this same simple but fundamental understanding of the complete management process.

One large and successful multinational corporation—International Minerals and Chemicals—found the chart of sufficient use and value to have it reproduced on the reverse side of all internal memorandum pads to serve as a constant reminder to all members of the management team about where any particular proposal they were working on would fit into the entire sequence of the management thinking process.

There is no reason why there should be any mystery about what that process is. Its elements and its sequence can be clearly identified and this can in turn permit clear individual identification with its purpose and its movement.

The Gardener's Approach to the Management of Thinking

Besides understanding clearly the thinking process of management, the leaders of organizations must also recognize that stimulants to the thinking process—and that process itself—are different for every person. Each individual mind, if it is going to be asked to think on behalf of the organization, should be integrated into the organizational thinking system with as much consideration and understanding of individual thinking differences as possible. In fact, the *productive* management of minds can and should be likened more to gardening than to commanding a military unit or running a manufacturing factory.

Like nature's plants, each mind has its own specific requirements for the equivalents of climate, soil, cultivation, nourishment and habits of growth and bearing fruit. An individual's mind cannot be *forced* to perform its thinking function; it can only be given the right conditions—motivation, discipline and care—and then be allowed to grow and flower. We all know that some minds work best early in the morning in isolation, quiet and order; others work best with noise and disorder; while others work best late at night. Consideration should be given to such individual variables in order to eliminate some of the barriers to the optimum functioning of the organization's mind, so that each individual can be encouraged to play the instrument of his mind as best he can.

In addition to creating an organizational environment that accepts individual differences in approaches to thinking, there are three other important ways for management to help eliminate organizational barriers to effective thinking and to convey the gardener's approach to individual minds within the organization:

—Communicating a sense of purpose
—Motivation and rewards
—Creating an environment of tolerance for thinking

Communicating a Sense of Purpose

An individual can be motivated only if his thought and work are important to him *personally,* as well as to the organization. Most human beings will work and think well only when they find value or purpose in their task. Effective thinking is the first casualty of an environment where, although there is discipline, there is no sense of purpose. In such cases, individual talents are often directed toward developing ingenious ways to avoid the discipline and "beat the system."

Communicating a sense of purpose is therefore an important first step toward stimulating and integrating the various individual parts of the mind of the organization into an effective whole. A clear sense of purpose should ultimately lead to a rewarding individual identification both with the successful organizational results and with the effective contribution of the individual to those results. Recognition of these contributions closes the loop, as "purpose achieved" becomes part of the reward for efforts expended on the "purpose sought."

Motivation and Rewards

Management must *clearly* provide incentives, promotions and recognition as compensation to capable individuals for their efforts and the risks they take in *both* thinking and acting on behalf of the organization. Offering attractive career programs for people in staff and R&D positions is one method of dealing with the problem. A more fundamental approach is to improve the methods of presenting thinking assignments—a subject to be further developed in Chapter 9.

Creating an Environment of Tolerance for Thinking

Management cannot of course tolerate poor performance in the final judgment/decision stage of the thinking process. But in the first three stages it *must* tolerate and welcome ideas which may later be rejected in order to generate a sufficient number of alternatives and insights into the future on which to base a sound decision.

The fact that some ideas will be accepted and some rejected as a *normal* part of the organizational thinking process should be recognized by all concerned. Unfortunately it seldom is. Individual thinkers, however, in order to be effective, *must* be assured within reason that unaccepted alternatives will not be used as a basis for assigning blame or ridicule, or for short-circuiting career development. The indispensable kind of mental free play which can generate creative, useful ideas will inevitably also produce some "waste" products. This is natural and should be accepted with a positive attitude by management and by all individuals who think as a contributing part of the mind of the organization.*

* It is important to take at least passing note of the many forms in which, under the loosely applied label of "industrial democracy," organized employee influence is beginning to work its way into the

The thinking process of an organization is a serious subject that responsible management should take seriously. And the acceptance of the above attitudes—reflecting the gardener's approach—is the first step, in our view, that needs to be taken by management in order to demonstrate to all concerned that it does indeed take the subject seriously.

The observations in the last two chapters have attempted both to identify some of the more important internal organizational barriers that often prevent the organization's mind from performing effectively, and to determine some of the basic management *attitudes* that need to be adopted to overcome these barriers. We now wish to look at some specific practical operating procedures and practices that should be adopted by management—if a *serious* organizational effort to produce better decisions is to be attempted. These proposals will assume that management has already recognized that its organization does have a mind, and that the needs of that mind for a sense of purpose, motivation and security must be served.

---

management decision-thinking process. This influence is being felt in quite a range of forms from the legal requirement in some western countries, such as West Germany, that fixed proportions of Board positions must be selected by trade unions to the many established labor-management committees set up to deal with specific employee problems and complaints.

It is not our purpose in this writing to speculate on the problems or the timing involved in a change from the adversary positions that have so long characterized labor-management relationships in organizations. However, it seems quite clear that not only these relationships are changing but that the old distinctions between owners, management, labor, consumers and the general public are beginning to disappear with a growing recognition that there exists a much larger community of "stake-holders" who share *common* interests in the responsible and productive functioning of any organization.

9

Twelve Practical Procedures to Improve
the Effectiveness of the Organization's Mind

> The various functions which make up an organization are always mediated by the interactions of people, so that the organization can never escape its human processes. As long as organizations are networks of people, there will be processes occurring between them. Therefore, it is obvious that the better understood and better diagnosed these processes are, the greater will be the chances of finding solutions to . . . problems which will be accepted and used by the members of the organization.
>
> Edgar H. Schein, *Process Consultation: Its Role in Organization Development*

Effective thinkers and the proper organization of thinkers are important corporate assets which need to be cultivated with care if management is to deal skillfully with the problems it faces. Once management accepts this view and understands that its organization does possess a brain *and* a mind—on both of which the well-being of the organization depends—then the following are some of the more important practical steps that can be taken by management to increase the value of these thinking assets* and to build an effective thinking system within the organization.

* Many of the actions identified in this chapter may be followed by some organizations implicitly, but as we stated at the beginning of this book, we believe considerable benefit can be derived from being *explicit* about the processes of, and the demands to be made on, the organization's mind. There seems little to be gained in being vague about a subject that management does not need to be vague about.

1. A Commitment—Management should above all else openly declare and explicitly accept its responsibility for creating and maintaining an effective organizational thinking capability that follows the four-stage thinking process of the individual's mind.

   Once this is clearly understood by all members of the management team and by all the other individual contributors to the organization's mind, then management will have taken the single most important procedural step that it can to improve the thinking performance of its organization. Furthermore, by explicitly identifying the four-stage decision-thinking process for all individuals who contribute their thoughts to the mind of the organization, management will have established a common thinking framework so that thinking tasks can be more precisely and effectively assigned.

2. The assignment of thinking responsibilities must be explicit.

   It should be clear to all important decision-makers within the organization that two of their most fundamental responsibilities are (a) to carefully define and control the questions asked by them of the organization's mind; and (b) to ensure that alternative answers and their predicted consequences are being effectively and honestly generated by the individuals responsible. Reporting procedures should then be initiated so that management can be certain these responsibilities are being routinely met by the key decision-makers. Such procedures would include, for example, periodic reports to senior management on the most important questions each decision-maker is asking of his department or division, and on the important thinking tasks he has assigned internally and to outside advisors.

3. All important projects or assignments should clearly identify both the thinking and the action efforts required and assign responsibility for both accordingly. Projects which involve serious thought about a complicated corporate problem should be *deliberately* organized according to the four stages of the mind's thinking process. For example: "The purpose of this project (or this phase of the project) will be to develop the most intelligent and effective questions on the subject of . . . ," "The purpose will be to create alternative answers to the following question . . . ," or "We ask you to provide us with alternative answers, and your projections as to their consequences, to the following question. . . ."

4. The "meetings of minds" should also receive deliberate and careful attention.
   Management should ensure that all important problem-solving meetings are systematically organized— again according to the stage of the thought process involved. The first task should be to understand and define the problem/question to be asked of the individual minds in the meeting. This should be followed by a discussion to create or develop alternative solutions, with the analysis and prediction of their consequences to follow. A presentation of the various options developed should then be made in order that a decision selection can be taken. This entire process could all be covered in a single meeting or during several meetings, depending on the time available and the importance of the problem being considered.*

---

* The days and nights of meetings between top American government leaders during the "Cuban missile crisis," as publicly reported by various participants, are one dramatic example of how the best minds available were gathered to define a critical problem and to explore a range of options for action, with thoughtful speculation on the possible consequences of each alternative. This particular crisis

Furthermore, the invitations to attend meetings should be based on the specific purpose and subject agenda of the meeting, rather than simply on the authority status of the participants. The often-heard complaint of busy executives that "I seem to be spending all of my time at meetings" is frequently an indication that those people calling the meetings did not consider *which* stage in the decision-thinking process had been reached that required a meeting. For example, meetings of top-level "deciders" are often not productive for dealing with the *development* of new ideas, alternative solutions to problems or speculative measurements of possible consequences.

5. Management should clearly specify that the corporate planning activity is a product of the organization's mind.

Planning is a vital thinking activity of an organization, and therefore management should endeavor to ensure that it is recognized as such by all the individual minds within the organization's mind who are asked to contribute their thoughts to the planning process. A formal commitment to corporate planning *does* provide a framework within which organized attention can be given to the development of the organization's thinking function. The requirement to participate in the creation and development of a corporate plan can also serve as a productive introduction to the meaning of a thinking responsibility

---

is an example of a problem allowed to develop which then had to be reacted to—a common management failure to accurately plan or predict *before* something goes seriously wrong. But quite aside from any judgments as to why the problem was even allowed to develop, the reports on the series of meetings that did take place make an excellent case history of decision-thinking, one that would be of interest to any person having to orchestrate a "meeting of minds."

for those individuals selected for the first time to participate. Furthermore, if management can, from time to time, subject some of the organization's sacred cows to this planning process, it will have a major positive impact on the organization by demonstrating that management honestly values the thinking capabilities of its human resources.

6. Job descriptions, performance evaluations and recruitment announcements should, when relevant, include thinking responsibilities.

Statements of individual responsibilities should identify the thinking as well as the "doing" responsibilities. For example, the responsibility of certain individuals to generate new solutions to problems should be as clearly identified in job descriptions as is the management responsibility for making final decisions.

Furthermore, employees should be recruited primarily in certain instances according to the thinking functions that the organization will require of them. Where the ability to think creatively or analytically is essential to performance, such a capability should be a primary qualification for placement and promotion—and *clearly* identified as such to the individual being recruited.

7. A sympathetic tolerance must be developed within the organization for unaccepted ideas generated during the first three stages of the thinking process.

Again, it should be made very explicit by management to *all* contributors to the organization's mind that the initial three stages of the thinking process—questions, alternatives, and consequences—provide *indispensable* inputs for decision-making. New ideas plus applied information provide the raw material from which a decision is made. An "error" tolerance *prior* to the judgment stage should therefore be *deliberately* encouraged by management for all problem-solving or opportunity-creating meetings and projects—in order to develop a greater sense of freedom for an *honest* thinking effort by the organization's mind. And when ideas are rejected, the reasons for rejection should be made clear. In most practical terms, psychological barriers to offering proposals which may be rejected can often be removed by clearly noting in advance that certain discussions are to be "free wheeling" with the participants encouraged to "think out loud" about the subject at hand. Discussions under this type of deliberate encouragement often generate a certain amount of "chaff" that has little value other than as tension-easing humor, but they are a type of discussion that can bring forward partly formed ideas that can be hammered into sound proposals through the give and take of openly encouraged thinking and expression by the participants.

8. The organization's mind should be exposed deliberately from time to time to external stimulation.

The barriers to thinking within an organization that we have discussed in Chapter 7 will *always* be present in varying degrees. Therefore it may well be prudent or necessary to seek other sources of ideas from outside the organization, in order to find the fresh, creative thinking required to solve major problems. The deliberate seeking of sources of new options from outside the organization can become as meaningful a corporate practice as efforts to diversify sources of earnings or raw materials. The use of an outside set of minds is particularly valuable for breaking out of thinking patterns which may have become constricting forces on all the thinking efforts of the organization's mind. This does not mean that any outside group of minds is "better" or "smarter" than those within the organization. Bringing in outsiders as board members or advisors is merely a pragmatic method of management to learn whether there are more effective ways to look at a situation than those that seem most comfortable because they are most familiar.

9. Controls should be introduced for reviewing the organization's thinking procedures and activities.

Each decision-making center should be held responsible, once proper procedures are introduced, for being able to demonstrate at all times that its *thinking* processes, as well as its action and administrative processes, are in order. This could be done by reviewing, for example, the minutes of important meetings, the job evaluation sheets for key employees, and the procedures for giving out special assignments.

10. "Working smarter" reviews.

In addition, as a normal corporate discipline, key decision-makers should also *periodically* be asked to identify what specific steps they have taken to ensure that they and their departments are, as IBM puts it, "working smarter."

11. Organizational thinking should be guided by establishing a simple format for the presentation of proposals.

Executives should establish a simple format in which they *expect* to receive recommendations for decision and action. There is no point in having an organization that is effective in generating sound ideas unless these are presented in such a way that they *can* receive a fair hearing from the decision-makers.

The Appendix is included as an example of one

such format that was used effectively by an executive who found he was being forced to spend a great deal of time adjusting his own way of looking at problems to the widely varied methods of presenting proposals selected by his management team. From some parts of his organization he was receiving proposals and studies that seemed to represent the complete files of knowledge on the subject under consideration. The staff was saying in effect, "Look, boss, how hard we have worked and how much we know about this matter." Other proposals were statistically heavy, but with no effort made to evaluate these measurements relative to the original purpose of the study. Some were encumbered by the obscure polysyllabic language in which many experts communicate. In a word, his organization was *not* communicating with him in the terms he needed for his clear understanding of the problem on which his judgment and decision were being sought. When first introduced, the simple format shown in the Appendix proved to be much more than a change in an office procedure. It proved to be a most revealing tool for showing how completely haphazard and fragmented this executive's own organization was in thinking about corporate problems.

The design of procedures should serve the particular "perception skills" of the person receiving a proposal. These skills are quite varied. People "receive" information in different ways. Some executives, particularly those skilled in rapid reading, understand ideas best through written proposals. Others prefer oral presentations and discussions. Some are most comfortable with quantified data and say "I don't want your prose, your rhetoric or your judgments. Give me statistical measurements." (Robert S. McNamara, former U.S. Secretary of Defense, was well known as one such "numbers man.") Finally, there are those who say, "Give me a picture of your proposal" and mean it quite literally. They need visual presentations that show patterns representing situations, cost, size, time and trend relationships.

There is probably no more frustrating experience than that of developing a "sure-fire" proposal and then having it rejected or ignored because, in the view of the author of the proposal, it was not properly understood or did not receive adequate attention. It is management's responsibility to let an organization know how it best receives proposals. A message is not communicated until it has been received, and all concerned parts of the organization must therefore learn to recognize the perception skills of the executives they serve. There is seldom any lack of critical observation about the ability of an executive to understand an issue on which he has acted unfavorably or not at all. It is rare, however, for such critics even to consider that they may have sent a garbled message, or one that was not well tuned to the reception capabilities and predilections of the receiver.

12. There should be internal or external auditing procedures established to evaluate the thinking practices of an organization.

To ensure that most of the above recommendations are implemented, and that the organization's mind *does* follow the four-stage system of man's own mind, specialists trained in organizational thinking procedures (probably a new profession) should be employed or called in from outside the organization from time to time to evaluate for management the organization's thinking performance, and to make recommendations on how the individual parts of an organization's mind can be made to think together more effectively.

Careful and conscientious attention to the above twelve recommendations—as well as application of the same kind of attention to the gardener's approach to the organization's mind called for in the previous chapter—can, we are persuaded, increase the *probability* of management's making more effective and rewarding decisions. We believe these recommendations can also help break down such barriers to the proper functioning of the organization's mind as *the risk of waste, the risk of rejected thinking, the dislike of uncertainty, the desire for action* and *the stifling influence of hierarchy and controls.*

Our proposals represent only initial steps for improving the performance of the organization's mind, but they are, we believe, steps in the right direction. In due course additional and more sophisticated organizational thinking practices will undoubtedly be developed by organizations and by students of the individual mind and the decision-thinking process of management. Although some executives may find even these initial steps too radical or too difficult to implement, we believe that they are all necessary *if* a serious and responsible effort is to be attempted by any management team to improve the decision-making capabilities of its organization.

10

Conclusion

Man's individual mind *and* the collective mind within an organization are the *primary* tools with which mankind can attempt to solve the great and growing problems that we face today and will face in the future. These minds produce the inputs for the decision-thinking processes which direct the activities of the organizations that guide most of the forces affecting our lives. For this reason alone, the time has now come when we must focus as much attention on the mind of the organization as we have over the last forty years on the brain of the organization.

The mind of an organization consists of the individual minds of its members *and the system* in which these individual minds *interact* and *interdepend* as a group to develop concepts for future action. To understand how this collective mind works, we need first to understand the decision-oriented thought processes of the thinking system of the individual human mind. But mere understanding is not enough.

We will also need to have responsible executives concerned with making their organizations perform more effectively who recognize far more clearly than they have heretofore that one of the most important elements in their organization's resource mix is the *thinking* capability of its human resources. By so doing, they can then do a great deal to improve the effectiveness of their organization's own collective thinking effort by skillfully developing formal and informal procedures and attitudes that will foster more pro-ductive thinking.

We have offered our observations and recommendations on a complex and important subject—the relationship between the decision-thinking process of man's individual mind and the decision-thinking process of the mind of the organization. A great deal has been written dealing in depth with certain aspects of what we have discussed. But for a decision-maker, the realization that his organization *does* have a mind—composed of individual minds that do possess a thinking system that identifies, creates and answers questions—and that this mind of the organization can be stimulated to function with greater order and effectiveness by instituting organizational practices that follow *and* respect the four-stage question-answering thinking process of man's individual mind, is, we believe, a useful and timely perception.

Part Two

The Polaris Missile Management Story

A case history of how an organization's mind was successfully created, sustained and employed.

On December 2, 1955, Admiral Arleigh A. Burke, then Chief of United States Naval Operations, issued a top-secret letter to his senior staff, establishing the priority that had been given by President Eisenhower for the development of a U.S. naval weapon system that would permit the launching of long-range nuclear warhead missiles from ships and submarines at sea. This fundamental decision led to the creation of the organization to be discussed herein.

The development program was officially known as the Fleet Ballistic Missile Program, but became more commonly known as the Polaris Program. This name was taken from the first in a series of long-range ballistic missiles around which the whole naval weapon system was to be built.

During the past two decades, the program moved successfully through three improved versions of the Polaris missile; it then made a major advance in 1970 to the Poseidon missile; and it is currently developing the awesome Trident missile submarine system.

A 1975 review of the accomplishments of this program showed that a Fleet Ballistic Missile capability existed in the first line of the nation's strategic deterrence containing major elements:

— Forty-one nuclear-powered ballistic missile submarines, armed with Polaris A-3 and Poseidon missiles, and deployed in all oceans of the world
— Four supporting ships and two overseas bases to maintain operations in all oceans of the world
— Two assembly facilities and four personnel training sites

The existence of this fleet of nuclear-powered submarines, capable of launching long-range ballistic missiles at targets in any country which might attack the United States, and with nuclear warheads powerful enough to destroy such an enemy from all oceans of the world, has served and continues to serve its purpose as a forceful deterrent to any war directly involving the major world powers.

The organization managing the development of the Fleet Ballistic Missile Program for over two decades has involved the participation of over twenty thousand large and small contractors, as well as many government agencies and universities. The basic management concepts established to develop the first Polaris A-1 missiles launched from the submarine USS George Washington on July 20, 1960, have continued to stand the test of time as the Program has moved forward through many improvements in the following years, without major alteration.

This particular case history has been included in this book to illustrate for the reader how one of the largest, most significant and complex management tasks in modern history was successfully handled by creating, cultivating and continually using the mind of an organization. As an applied practical example of abstract theory, it illustrates, we believe, how specific management actions may be taken to ensure that a complex, multibillion-dollar effort can be successfully managed continually with the cooperation and contributions of thousands of individual minds, representing a wide range of specialist skills.

While it is strange that many people fail to learn from their own mistakes and those of others, it is even more strange that examples of success often seem to have such little impact on the behavior of others. It is always easier to ascribe the success of others to factors not apparently available to oneself than to look for the comparable resources that are available with which to achieve similar success. The Polaris Program was managed by talented people, but they were not unusually gifted in any way. Unusually talented people, on balance, are evenly distributed around the world, including those who staff business and government organizations. But the Polaris organization learned to develop and use the potential talents of its "average" human resources to achieve outstanding results. This effort is a striking example of the basic thesis of this book concerning the potentials of an organization's mind when its individual human components are stimulated by opportunities for disagreements and challenged by claims on imaginative proposals. Out of the commonly motivated minds and disciplined dialogue that became the "ordinary" approach to problem discussions in the Polaris Program flowed decisions that proved to be completely effective.

Although the management of the Polaris Program did not specifically identify in practice the concept of the mind of the organization, the four-stage thinking process of man's mind was the implicit thinking framework for the management of the Program and therefore crucial to its success. Furthermore, as we will point out, management did in practice pay careful attention at all times to the thinking processes and thinking efforts that were required to make the Polaris Program a success. The management of the Polaris

Program did not identify itself as or consider itself to be a "think tank," in the pattern of various groups which exist to work on quite hypothetical or speculative problems and to offer measured alternative solutions to such problems. The problems and opportunities in the Program were real. They continually required action-oriented decisions. The Polaris organization did not have a "musing mind." It created a systematic decision-thinking process that now has been in operation for over twenty years.

The Special Management Approaches of the Program

Among the specific new management approaches influenced by the Polaris Program experience, the following six seem most important:

First, at the center of the Polaris Program was a small Navy agency specifically charged with management of the total Program. This agency was known simply as the Special Projects Office. There were also specific counterpart organizations operating in many of the offices of the contracting firms. The entire complex of participants was held together by a communications and planning network, which permitted all of the parts, at all levels of the work, to function together in a decision-thinking process.

The establishment of the Special Projects Office within the Navy Department to administer the Polaris Program was at that time a major innovation in organizational structure for project management by a government department. The appointment to this office of a Director who was broadly chartered in his responsibilities for being right in his decisions, but also strongly supported in his authority to be wrong, was a key early decision. Much that has since been done in the organization and management of research and development projects, and more broadly defined programs in the Defense Department, finds an antecedent root in this Special Projects Office of the Navy.

Second, the Polaris Program was one of the most widely used and successful applications of the *systems approach* to

1. Defining the content and problems of a large program.
2. Dimensioning the effort required to resolve complex and interrelated technical and nontechnical problems.
3. Organizing the productive skills of many disciplines toward the solution of tasks.
4. Most importantly, providing the motivation, programs and planning procedures by which thousands of minds could think systematically together toward solving practical problems.

Dr. Stark Draper of MIT once encapsulated this last point in his observation that the approach to the Polaris Program showed "that the theoretical approach is often the most practical. Or, when all else fails—Think."

Third, the Polaris management approach provided an early and important example of what is now called "cost-benefit analysis," and of how this type of analysis can be the foundation for major decisions concerning important long-term objectives. The total benefits to be achieved from successful accomplishment of the objectives in this program were measured against the total costs of gaining these same advantages by other means. The objectives were to obtain an invulnerable strategic striking force that would serve as a deterrent to any nuclear attack on the United States, and would exist as an available counterforce even *after* any such attack had been launched. In these terms the total costs involved were considered against the savings that would be realized by *not* attempting to achieve the same objectives through other equally expensive and less effective programs then under way. Thus, the discontinuance of work on other large-scale intercontinental ballistic missile and long-range bomber programs was an easily measured potential saving in the cost-benefit arithmetic that was worked into the judgment and decision equations of the Defense Department.

Fourth, much that was developed in connection with the management of the Polaris Program has influenced the approach to managing other large development programs during the past twenty years. One of the major scheduling, performance control and planning techniques first developed by the management of the Polaris Program and known as the "performance evaluation and review technique" (PERT) has now become a universal tool with an almost unlimited number of widely different applications in various forms. PERT helped to make possible the integration of the thinking processes of the entire management structure and was one of the vitally important means for creating the organizational mind of the Polaris Program.

Fifth, another important element of the Polaris management story was the planned publicity and exposure of its management techniques, aimed at educating the Program's participants and at motivating the many people whose support was required. These people had to be convinced that the complex program was being well managed, and that assurances of ultimate success were firmly based on continuously measured and meaningful progress.

Sixth, and essential to a proper understanding of the above points, is that the management of the elements of such a program to achieve defined time and performance *objectives* was of pivotal importance. A great deal of what was learned in this experience has since been translated into the planning, programing and budgeting requirements of many government agencies, and has also found its way into corporate planning procedures. This experience has also helped develop the concept of "management by objectives," for without objectives, there can be no meaningful measurements of activity and accomplishments.

The Special Constraints

Business organizations are profit-oriented and should be concerned with obtaining the greatest possible results from their financial and human assets. They should be concerned with goal achievement at the lowest realistic cost possible. This means efficiency, and the greatest source of efficiency is careful and effective planning. The Polaris Program demanded efficiency because complicated and far-reaching goals were to be attained while at the same time budgetary and other restraints or constraints were imposed. Efficiency through planning, therefore, was paramount.

All decision-thinking systems operate under identifiable and sometimes special constraints. Frequently an organization finds it does not have enough money with which to act on "best solutions," however thoughtfully arrived at. Minds in such organizations often become weary of working on "make do" answers. Other minds, of course, in the same situation find it quite stimulating. If you do not have million-dollar bills to throw at your problems, you just have to think harder, and this can be more personally satisfying.

Other organizations operate under the opposite constraint of having too much money. The "cost plus a percentage of cost fee" contract has a built-in disincentive to thinking about better ways of doing anything—except, of course, ensuring that these lucrative contracts are renewed. Many public utilities operate with rate structures and escalation clauses of the same basic character that contain disincentives to thinking.

Other companies, and they are identifying themselves with increasing vigor on the American scene, operate under

the constraint of excessive and obsolete government regulations that effectively deny them any purpose in thinking
about improving their operations. Such companies either
accommodate themselves in comfort or frustration to these
types of constraints, or try to break out of their role as "state
wards" by extending their activities into areas that still
permit enterprise to operate with some freedom to succeed.

We could identify many other commonly recognized constraints known to many corporations, but our purpose in
this section is to give some understanding of the real world
of this case history.

There were inherent constraints in the management of
the Polaris Program which are not always present in managing R&D efforts.

Time was the first constraint. Time had a measured value
in the Program. The impact of the Russian Sputnik success
and the concern over a "missile gap" dictated much of the
time pressure on the Program in its first years. Two years
were cut off a five-year schedule in response to this pressure,
even though the normal time estimated to develop the
weapon system in the pattern of other projects was originally
ten years to produce the first submarine with missile-launch-
ing ability. The managers of the Polaris Program did not
have the luxury of unlimited time in which to follow interesting scientific and technical possibilities which at best would
have had only long-term payoff. Such efforts were authorized
on a limited scale, but they were clearly recognized to have
only second- and third-generation value in the time scale of
priorities.

The constraint of time, making this a "crash program,"
had both negative and positive values in relation to program
management. On the negative side, it was claimed that it
was not possible to do research on time schedules, and that
effort on a crash basis would always end up taking more
time than when the job was done the way it should be. This

was a deeply felt opinion, expressed by responsible men who were being asked to perform seemingly impossible tasks. Much that is in the management story of the Polaris Program provided answers to this fundamental objection.

In response to this first objection, concerning time limitations, it was necessary to draw the important distinction between discovery and invention. A distinction had to be made between research planned to result in new discoveries of previously unknown facts, and research oriented toward invention-making something through thought and experimentation. No effort was made to schedule discovery, although some research, it was hoped, would also lead to breakthroughs in many fields. This was basic research. No time objectives were related to such possibilities. But invention was scheduled! This was considered to be a matter that would lend itself to the organization of resources and creative extrapolation from progress in the "state-of-the-art" as applied research.

As to the second objection, concerning the inadequacies of what might be invented, it was also recognized that there would be a calculated risk in seeking a quick first success. Where feasible, backup effort was initiated to cover part of this risk. The impact of failure was assessed in the context of the total Program time objectives by means of the PERT information system of scheduling and reporting progress. This system was in fact one of the brain activities of the Polaris Program in the sense in which we have earlier referred to the brain of the organization.

There were also important advantages to planning and working under time pressure. Management was forced to give first-priority attention to the decision-thinking and planning processes which brought matters up for decision. As has been noted, there was disciplined attention to this responsibility which followed the four-stage thinking process we have described. So much that goes wrong in "crash programs" is due simply to the fact that the time pressures are all pushed onto the "doers" in an organization, and few are accepted by the "deciders." In the Polaris Program, when it became clear that management was doing its job "on time," the productive energies of everybody else in the organization responded positively to this lead by sharing an equitable burden of pressure.

Time pressure also made it necessary for management to make decisions in terms of a total impact. For example, if lack of a critical component from one source resulted in expensive down-time delay at another point, such as the lack of a pump delaying a major submarine construction schedule, additional cost and effort to speed up work on the pump was quickly authorized. This rather simple piece of good management may seem quite obvious. Yet, under much of current government or business audit control, it is often much easier to accept the small and auditable saving of a competitively bid supply item and ignore the much larger but nonauditable expenses from delayed performance by another contractor dependent on a delinquent supplier. The pressure of Program time values forced management to take actions based on the broader and more efficient view. (If the Polaris Program had failed, the auditors would probably still be crawling all over the record highlighting nickel-and-dime so-called "waste" in auditable items.)

A second constraint on the Polaris design and development effort was the simple one of having to work with the *physical size* of a submarine. This constraint is certainly not peculiar to submarine systems. It also applies to most ships and aircraft. But it was an important specific constraint which forced the most careful attention to all aspects of the total operational system. The managers of the Program were required to think about all matters in relationship to the physical operational environment of a submarine. This consideration included not only the "hardware" design and performance decisions, but also the whole range of operational requirements. It included, for example, basic human engineering design decisions such as selection of crew skills and numbers in relation to on-board spares and maintenance and repair functions.

These considerations may seem obvious in retrospect. They were certainly very evident in the careful planning of the American space program. Yet, this type of total operational system thinking is a comparatively recent novelty in the history of defense research and development.

A third constraint was the *requirement for functional accuracies* that stretched the meaning of quality control beyond anything previously required. Management had to recognize an order-of-magnitude increase in the requirement for perfect performance. Where functional redundancy and backup systems could be provided, this was done, but much of the rest of the system had to work perfectly one time— the first time. There was at that time no pilot or ground control that could correct in-flight error once the missile had been launched.

This constraint was recognized early in the Program, and new procedures for discipline and training were required to ensure adequate quality control. In this instance, the Program managers and their contractors had to learn these new lessons together. (The lessons learned added to the sum total of new knowledge that now exists to support government-directed research and development activity.)

Finally, there was the relatively unique constraint of *great public interest*. The Program was started during the days of the much publicized "missile gap." As one of the many missiles which were being introduced in the early years of the Program, the Polaris test firings at Cape Canaveral were important news. This was long before the days of success, of well-organized publicity programs and of television audiences which have grown accustomed to seeing men walk on the moon. As so much of the test program had high visibility, it was not only necessary to be right in this work, it had to look right. A large rocket that explodes in full view makes a spectacular news picture, and, in those days of critical concern, such an event made an easy story of "failure." The Polaris management had to carry part of the burden of educating the public to the sophistication of test programs in which "failure" is sometimes planned in order to acquire a certain test result. Polaris management accepted this "fact of life" and gave the matter the attention it properly deserved.

The Objective

The Polaris Program was set up in late 1955 to develop a fleet ballistic missile capability. The emphasis here is on the last word—"capability." A decision was made at the highest executive levels of government that it was desirable to have a capability to launch long-range ballistic missiles from sea-borne platforms. It was from that decision that all that followed was derived. The first effort was to adapt the Army Jupiter missile to a surface ship. There have since been many major phases of improvement in the Program, culminating in today's Trident missile, which, with its greater range and target selection capability, can open even greater areas of the world's oceans in which submarines can conceal their presence and allow missiles to penetrate the most sophisticated defense systems of a potential attacking country.

The Polaris Program was not merely an effort to develop a new weapon system that seemed technically feasible, which if proved might then be used in some larger plan. The objective was to create a military capability. This point is significant to every aspect of this case history.

For example, a great deal of the necessary research and development for the Program was recognized as a *phase* through which progress would have to be made. The R&D effort in the Polaris Program kept its identity as a phase of a defined military capability effort, and did not lose its primary focus by being lumped with all other defense research and development efforts and then buried with the separately reviewed and considered R&D programs of the Defense Department and the Navy. The Polaris R&D effort established and kept its identity throughout as a critical phase of a defined military capability project.

Other parts of the Program also maintained their particular focus and identity. The entire range of effort, including production, testing, maintenance, supply, facility construction, and personnel selection and training, were all considered as phases and parts of a total weapon system capability program. It was recognized that the capability being sought was that of a total system with many interrelated parts—not merely the creation of hardware, but also the selection and training of men to maintain and operate the weapon system, the complete range of operational and logistic supporting elements (such as tender support, communications, overseas bases, maintenance and overhaul facilities), as well as operational doctrine. All of these interrelated positions were elements of what was known as the "Program Package."

If this military model seems a bit exotic and removed from corporate business reality, consider the parallels with any mining company, for example, which must first complete its geological findings, then in turn build the mine and processing facilities, develop transportation to market, train personnel and, in many cases, even provide complete community facilities for a work force as well as design and develop marketing strategies in order to make a mine profitable. The functional interdependencies that exist in *all* corporate life differ from the Polaris example only perhaps in scale and historical significance.

The Program

The importance of having a *meaningful* program to manage was primary. It would be quite wrong, however, to suggest that while a decision had been made about the desired end result, the full content of the effort required was immediately identified. The Polaris Program content evolved in part through new technological proposals, but also, as time went by, quite simply through a growing understanding of the many things that were required to provide the desired capability. These revised value judgments were incremental and dynamic in relation to time projections, size of Program and new performance potentials which were revealed as the work progressed.

At the beginning, there was a great practical hazard in presenting a total Program Package for approval. The price tag was high. Since the Navy's resources were not unlimited, this meant that money would have to be diverted from other projects—a prospect not well received by other naval project managers. Yet, this high price tag was very deliberately revealed by the *proponents* of the Program from its earliest days. Given the usual fragmented approach to funding defense efforts in those earlier days, the Program might never have been started if the top decision-makers had not believed in the potential value of success and had a strong desire to define an objective large enough from the start to justify the major management effort needed to do the job. In those days, funding decisions ordinarily were made under *departmental* budgetary ceilings strongly influenced by formula and historical pattern, and the Polaris Program had to find its funding within a Navy budget which at that time did not even have a claim on the Defense Department's "strategic mission" funds. In this budgetary environment the decision to hold the Program Package together, with its large price tag clearly stated, was indeed an act of great courage and conviction by many persons in and out of uniform at the top levels of the U.S. defense administration.

A well-defined program with carefully evaluated objectives gave a meaningful answer to the "Why" question, which is the first answer that management must have before it goes on to ask the mind of its organization to answer the questions of "Who, How, When, What and Where." Furthermore, without a sound answer to the "Why" question, subsequent criticism or compliments on how a job is done are quite irrelevant. We repeat an earlier observation that what is not worth doing is not worth doing well. Unfortunately, the record of Defense Department research and development, as indeed with much human effort, is replete with many cases of successful effort producing virtually useless results. This is sometimes referred to by R&D project managers as "the paradox of success."

It is, of course, meaningless to ascribe a value to an objective without prior consideration of its feasibility. For the Polaris Program, the availability of the medium-range Jupiter missile was the basis for proposing significant extension of its range by making a ship at sea the "first stage" of this missile. And, with the value of a ship-launched, long-range missile capability clearly appreciated, it was possible to develop a program of technological invention. Fascination with the technical accomplishments of the original effort was, when necessary, objectively set aside in order to find a better way to reach the *total* objective. For example, the entire structure of the effort associated with the adaptation of the Jupiter missile to ship-launch was subsequently halted in favor of building a newly feasible system that could operate from nuclear *submarines*, with a solid-fueled missile carrying a small guidance package and small but powerful nuclear warheads.

Many such decisions resulted from a systematic program

of question posing and question answering, deliberately applied throughout the project to the various component parts of the mind of the Polaris organization.

The Management of Thinking

The Polaris Program Director was responsible for coordinating and managing the total thinking and action effort of the organization. He directed a large part of the effort, but he was also responsible for planning and coordinating supporting work which he did not direct. In this instance, *coordination* was a strong word. It did not merely mean appeals to cooperate. It meant that he had the authority to *require* coordinated activity.

The other major elements of the Polaris decision-thinking approach were based on the "Why, When, Where, Who and How" questions. The "Why" question was answered for the Program by defining objectives with clearly established defense values. The "When" and "Where" questions were answered with the tight and then still further shortened work and production schedules of the Program. The large "Who" and "How" questions were basically answered with the decision to establish a Special Projects Office.

Questions and Answers

From the start of the project, hard value questions were asked and answered by the organization in the process of making both goal-oriented and technical decisions. For example, a basic set of questions was *continually* being asked not only in consideration of original design proposals, but also as part of the ongoing thinking effort required in the management review of progress and change. These questions, simply stated, were the following:

1. What is the problem or opportunity to which a proposal applies and what is being proposed? The problem and answer could apply to any part of the Program (hardware, personnel or logistic and operational support). This was the starting point of all proposal review.
2. What alternatives have been considered and rejected in arriving at this particular proposal, and why were they rejected?
3. How does the proposal fit the existing design parameter decisions already made? This question focused attention on the real value of the constraints already established. If, for example, a proposal for an important new piece of ship navigation equipment would require a reallocation of submarine space, it was realized that a design parameter would have to be redrawn.
4. What time or performance value will the proposed item add to the total system?
5. How is the proposed item to be provided? Is it within the existing or projected state of the art? Can its development be completed within the time period required to meet Program objectives?
6. How is performance of the proposed item to be proved? What are the criteria for the test program?
7. How much will the proposed item cost? (This question involved total resource costs, including man skills, time and facilities capacity as well as funds.)

In the beginning, an effort was made to formally document all proposals in response to these questions. This question-answering approach was applied to all aspects of the project. Although some of the problems might seem quite trivial, they were not so considered. A few examples will illustrate:

—What size bunks should be installed in the submarines? Standard? The answer was "No, we can do better than that. We must conserve space on board but every man must have a bunk that fits him. Check the probable distribution of heights among a normal complement of current submariners and we will provide for at least that amount of difference in bunk sizes."

—What sort of movies should be provided for submarines on patrol? The best? The answer selected was "No," as recommended by the Program's advising psychologist. "Run in some real 'dogs' on the movie schedule. There is nothing better than watching a bad movie to let the men get rid of any built-up hostilities after a long period of confined living."

—How shall we designate the different crews who rotate on patrol assignments? Should we use numerical or alphabetical sequence systems? The answer was "No, we will use color code designations that carry no suggestion of first team, second team or so forth. Each crew has an equal status and must have equal competence to take a ship on patrol."

Each question was considered in the broadest possible framework, and alternative courses of action were carefully examined. Sometimes two or even three alternatives were followed until the best one was proved to be right. The other alternatives were then abandoned or tailored for more modest "backup" support.

The importance of answering each unknown was assessed and the size of the effort to find that answer was related to its place in the overall successful program. Technological proposals were discussed only when they could be specifically related to defined time and performance goals.

Thus, the practice of being sure each proposal debated was based on relevant questions of value and purpose was of critical value to the decision-thinking process of the Polaris project.

It was soon learned, however, that the questions and answers could be given more meaningful consideration by direct *verbal* discussion at all levels rather than by establishing complex and time-consuming documentary procedures at the proposal stage. The highest level of such specific collective verbal thinking that first took place on project matters was in the Steering Task Group. This Group consisted of senior representatives from the prime contractors, from government agencies directly involved in the Program, from university research laboratories and from the military customers who would use the system, as well as members of the technical staff of the Special Projects Office. The agenda of these Steering Task Group meetings dictated that the particular representatives in attendance bring knowledge and relevant ideas with them to the meetings, rather than merely the authority of position.

After only three months of deliberations, the Steering Task Group made its original recommendations, which were approved by the Director. These decisions established technical performance goals in each area of development and dictated that the components be integrated into a working system at a specified future time. Future information, in terms of extrapolated, state-of-the-art potential, was added to varied past and present experience. This approach created one outstanding difference between Polaris and many other weapon programs, where the weapon, once successfully produced, is obsolete at the time of its first use. Anticipated general and specific technological advances were incorporated in basic design target decisions.

From these basic decisions, the various management systems and subsystems were developed. The Steering Task Group continued to meet throughout the initial Polaris Program as major decisions were required.

Supportive thinking efforts and decisions on lesser matters were made at principal contractor locations, and between prime contractors and subcontractors. Thus, it was of great importance for the Polaris Program that at all levels and for all proposals there existed a system of simple but relevant questions to be asked and answered, with continual reference to the time and performance objectives of the overall project.

The Special Projects Office

This Office was set up to be part of the administrative structure of the former Bureau of Naval Ordnance, but a direct line of accountability was drawn between the Director of the Office, the Chief of Naval Operations and the Secretary of the Navy in his capacity as Chairman of the Navy Ballistic Missile Committee.

Exhibit B presents an outline of the position of the Special Projects Office in the total government apparatus. The Director of the Special Projects Office could go directly to the centers of higher authority for discussion of his problems and accomplishments, and in search of approval for Program content and expansion.

The internal structure of the Special Projects Office was quite simple, as shown. Technical problems were assigned to a Division Director. The Technical Director substructured his division into branch groupings which reflected the major components of the weapon system itself. A second Division Director was designated Program Planning and Control Officer. His responsibilities covered four main areas:

1. Planning the overall thrust of the Program toward a fleet ballistic missile capability, or, more directly, *defining* "where we were going."
2. Determining "where we are" from a *review* of the continuous inflow of performance information.

EXHIBIT B

THE ORGANIZATION OF THE SPECIAL PROJECTS OFFICE IN THE GOVERNMENT CHAIN OF COMMAND

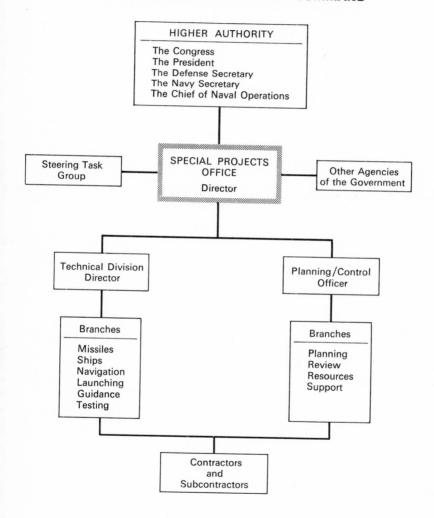

HIGHER AUTHORITY

The Congress
The President
The Defense Secretary
The Navy Secretary
The Chief of Naval Operations

Steering Task
Group

**SPECIAL PROJECTS
OFFICE**

Director

Other Agencies
of the Government

Technical Division
Director

Planning/Control
Officer

Branches

Missiles
Ships
Navigation
Launching
Guidance
Testing

Branches

Planning
Review
Resources
Support

Contractors
and
Subcontractors

3. Obtaining and managing the *resources* of the Program
   —funds, manpower, material and facilities.
4. Dealing with the *supporting* agencies outside of the
   Projects Office on such matters as military personnel
   training, communication facilities and supply support
   systems.

The Special Projects Office was not a new agency. Instead
it was a unique approach to establish a new center of authority that was to operate within the existing organization
of the Navy Department. The Director was given priority
claim on the resources of the Navy to accomplish his tasks.
He was enjoined not to duplicate any resources that could
already be found in the existing bureaus, offices and field
establishment of the Navy. This proved to be a wise but
difficult decision to administer. It required the most skilled
personal leadership to balance the elements of persuasion,
pressure and priority rights to elicit support from other divisions of the Navy. While this case study does not deal with
personalities, it should be noted that this type of organizational approach places the highest premium on a director or
chief executive with a mature personality and those unique
qualities of leadership that can secure the participation of
people who do not operate in a direct command or management line relationship. Such leadership was found in the
person of Rear Admiral W. F. Raborn.

The subsequent management answers to the "Who" and
"How" questions also involved significant changes from
prior practice regarding contractor roles in weapon development. The letting of a contract is an act of organization
decision, since it determines who will do a certain job. The
first decision that the Program Director had to make related
to the role of the Special Projects Office in the management
of the Polaris Program. This was a key decision. The Office

was not to be merely a fund-gathering and fund-disbursing agency for the Program, with a large prime contractor being given the task of overall Program leadership. The requirements of the Program for coordination with other government agencies meant that the idea of selecting a private company or a group of companies to pull together the total effort was quickly set aside. The Special Projects Office was to be the organizer of the total effort—the central management focus for the Program. It was to be both the command intelligence center and the command post in its relation to all supporting efforts.

The decision to run the Program from inside the government required an equally clear decision as to what the Special Projects Office would *not* do. The most important part of this decision was that it would not engage its authority in decisions on how a job would be done by contractors. This was easy to decide but difficult to accept. There was much that had to be unlearned by some of the staff that was first recruited to the Special Projects Office. To illustrate this point, while the Navy had much technical skill in its trained personnel simply because the Navy had long been a technical service, the Special Projects Office resisted the temptation to design equipment, but limited its authority to review and approval of design proposals and judgments on their adequacy and relevance to the purpose of the Program. In the mind of the Polaris organization, the Special Projects Office served as the central focus for consideration of the total Polaris system requirements.

Decisions and the Role of the Director

Following the major organizational decision on the role of the Special Projects Office, the Director had four options for establishing centers of authority and decision-thinking points in the small central office that was set up. These options can be conveniently designated as "the four D's" of choice:

1. He could Decide. That is, he could make the decisions. This pattern of administration exists in many organizations. Very little happens in such organizations until "the boss" has made a decision.
2. He could Deputize. This means that the head office still makes the decisions, but as "the boss" is too busy to hand down all the decisions, he surrounds himself with deputies who act in his name and with his authority.
3. He could Delegate. This means that some part of the authority of the head office has been passed to another part of the organization, where it is exercised as a representative of "the boss." The act of delegation can be reversed and the authority withdrawn to the head office and from the delegate.
4. He could Define. This means that an area of responsibility and authority is identified as the logical place where decisions of a defined type should be made. If the person in charge of such an area fails to perform, he is replaced, but the definition of the area is not changed.

Decision-thinking and decision-making in the Polaris Program were based primarily on "defined" areas of authority where direct responsibility for producing a desired result could be assigned. However, as the overriding task of the entire Special Projects Office was to produce a totally integrated result, each such defined center of authority had the important collateral responsibility for supporting and monitoring the work going on in other centers of authority which interfaced with its work. This meant that there could be none of the common barriers to both planning and thinking efforts between organizationally defined parts working on defined tasks. As the objective was to produce a completely integrated and interdependent weapon system capability, the total organization *had* to think and work together as an interdependent unit. Organizational barriers could not be tolerated. Each center of branch and divisional authority accepted a basic core of direct responsibility, but recognized that it had an *equal* responsibility for supporting and influencing decisions in areas of authority assigned to others which related to its own schedules and performance.

The manner in which the Polaris Program became an interdependent thinking and working unit is the most important part of this case history. As pointed out previously, it illustrates the basic thesis of this book—that an organization does have a mind which can work effectively *if* management provides the correct procedures and the necessary incentives for its proper functioning. Perhaps the best way to illustrate this is by the quotation of parts of a key statement in which the management concept for the Polaris Program was outlined by the Director of the Program in the first year of operation. Management systems cannot be designed from textbook references to serve what are only vaguely defined organizational objectives. The rationale of the basic purpose of *any* management control system requires conceptual expression that will guide the design of the system and, most importantly, motivate compliance with the procedural disciplines of its operation. The statement which is quoted below was written to serve the special requirements of a weapon system development and production program. It served that specific purpose well. However, the reader might find it a useful reference for contrast with the total absence or general vagueness of any comparable statement that exists in his own organization as guidance for the design, installation and operation of a rationalized management system.

The Navy has military and civilian personnel qualified to give top level direction to the technical and support effort required to develop a Fleet Ballistic Missile System. A basic decision has been made to manage this project through coordination and supervision by a small Navy "Management Team" of the work assigned to industry and to other government agencies. This type of management role requires that the Special Projects Office (SP) establish a management control system that will ensure maximum integration of staff work to support the type of decisions which must be made at the SP level of responsibility.

It is now necessary that the elements of a completely integrated management control system be developed to obtain the full potential of the Management Center. This memorandum is an outline of the principles that must govern the functioning of the management system, geared to the needs of the program and to the concept of project office management. The following outline of responsibility relationships is a frame of reference for understanding the purposes to be served by a management control system:

1. My relations to higher authority.
2. My relations to staff.
3. Staff relations to me.
4. Staff lateral relationships.
5. Staff relations to others who are doing work for the Special Projects Office.

My Relations to Higher Authority

The authorities to whom I am responsible are interested in execution of the total Fleet Ballistic Missile Program. This means that any specific proposal which must be referred for approval, or any performance report to higher authority, must present facts in clear context with the whole program. Not only must the nature of specific proposals be described, but the purpose of proposals in relation to the other elements of the program must be clearly drawn. The present complete definition of the total program must be maintained. Our program will retain this identity and its present top priority status only if we are able to show the logical, necessary relationship of all parts of this whole in all dealings with higher authority —I must be able to reach down to any level of activity and find a plan and a performance report that logically and clearly can be related to the total job we have to do.

My Relations to Staff

In my relations to staff, I can best meet my responsibilities by reviewing and approving proposed plans and by reviewing performance in relation to approved plans. Only by this method will it be possible to establish the clear flow of documented direction that is essential to the success of this project in which there have been such large assignments of authority for decision-making to the Division and Branch levels, and to define the principal terms in which accountability for staff performance will be established.

In order that proposed plans will serve these purposes, they must meet certain basic criteria. Plans must have complete information as to description and purpose of work proposed. Time and resources required to do the work must be shown. The major phases or milestones through which work will be carried out must be presented in timed sequence in order that review of plans can include examination of the adequacy of means and time to serve the ends desired.

Any plan of proposed work must be logically relatable to other approved or proposed plans. These relationships must be established in terms of being an essential or more detailed part of a larger or more broadly drawn plan, and being a supporting action to other approved or proposed plans. By establishing the main core of my relations with staff effort in these terms a major problem of executive communication will have been solved.

Staff Relations to Me

A major element of this relationship involves information from staff on actions taken under approved plans, and performance following from these actions. On this matter, the following guidance is provided:

1. Weekly summary reports covering performance in each major work area are required. This means reporting on each major component of work in each Branch.
2. These reports are required at the regularly established weekly staff meeting and should be presented in two parts:
   (a) A summary evaluation of performance covering progress against approved plans; and
   (b) Highlight reporting of exceptions in performance (good or bad) as they relate to planned schedules and effort. These highlight statements should cover the nature of the problem or performance reported on, the effect of the item on approved plans with this effect traced to whatever level or into whatever area of planned effort that is involved, and the action that is proposed for dealing with the matter discussed.

Staff Lateral Relations

All inter-staff communication requires establishment of common frames of reference that will permit direct and simple tracing of the effect of performance facts on planned effort in all supported and supporting areas of planned work. Thus a common format of planning and scheduling work is as essential to inter-staff coordination of work as it is to the establishment of relationships between the several levels of management authority.

Staff Relations to Others Who Are Doing Work for the Special Projects Office

Weekly reporting by contractors on performance is required to provide the basic flow of facts to staff. The problem with which we must deal, however, involves more than the timeliness and frequency of reporting from contractors on performance. A more difficult problem involves the relevance of reported data to the use that must be made of it. Management of this large program by a small project office staff requires that the most careful discriminations be made between important and unimportant facts to be reported by contractors. The determination of what we "need to know" cannot be prescribed by formula, but it can be established by detailed planning in the terms set forth in earlier paragraphs of this memorandum. I expect that plans will be made in these terms at least down to the levels where work is assigned to specific contractors.

I have assigned [the Planning and Control Officer] the primary responsibility for developing in more detail the essential elements of a management control system that will reflect these concepts and meet the needs briefly outlined herein.*

PERT—Part of the Management's Thinking System

The PERT system evolved from the requirements set forth in this quoted guidance memorandum from the Director. It was a means by which the hundreds of thousands of interrelated developments in this massive program could be identified as to their nature, measured in terms of their probability of being accomplished and, most importantly, related to all dependent planned activity that required their previous accomplishment. In effect, just as an electrical engineer needs circuitry diagrams to wire a switch panel, the various Program managers needed a network diagram to follow the flow of progress along the many channels of interrelated effort.

---

* From a January 24, 1957, Staff Memorandum from the Director on Special Projects Office management of the Fleet Ballistic Missile Program. Gordon Pehrson, coauthor of this book, was the Planning and Control Officer during the first four years of the Polaris Program from 1956 to 1960.—B. H. and G. P.

The four phases of the PERT approach were developed as follows:

1. The first phase was a system simply to do a better job of identifying the interrelationships of various jobs in the total Program. An existing, cross-referencing staff approach had proved to be slow, awkward and incomplete. Better assurance was needed that *everything* affected by *any* event could be identified.
2. If this first job could be done, it would have value. But, if in addition to the simple identification of an existing relationship this relationship could be further defined in terms of cause and effect, and *measured* in units of time, this would have greater value. These evaluations were done by the PERT system and thereby saved difficult and time-consuming staff work.
3. With success in these first two phases, a third output of the PERT system was sought which would represent a real breakthrough. This was a method of looking ahead at all of the future scheduled events and identifying or forecasting the most difficult part of doing the total remaining job—as reflected in existing schedules and accumulating performance data.
4. Finally, a fourth possibility was put into the system design effort for the PERT system. If the third phase was to be made able to cope with the *uncertainties* of future time predictions, the question naturally arose whether it would be possible to *recognize* uncertainties and to introduce some probability measurements into the identification and predictions of the most difficult part. This "most difficult part" was identified as the "critical path," and this phrase is now even commonly used to describe systems of scheduling and control for managing problems less complex than those which dominated the Polaris Program. The most interesting

aspect of this fourth development was the recognition that the *prediction judgments* of the people working on the Program as to how long it would take them to do their jobs were indeed *facts*. These judgments as to time estimates were facts which could be handled in statistical terms of probability and produce valuable indicators and measurements for the Program managers. The scientists and engineers working on the Program also welcomed this approach to scheduling invention, because it recognized the *uncertainties* in their effort by introducing *probability* estimates into their mental forecasts of what might be accomplished.

All four phases of this system design effort were accomplished. Since then, the PERT system has had widespread adaptation to many scheduling problems. The successful U.S. space program was one outstandingly successful application of PERT to an effort of comparable size. Most major and many minor construction projects in all parts of the world today also include PERT-like scheduling network controls.

Yet, in its application to the Polaris Program management, PERT was much more than a somewhat complicated computer-based, statistically valued network scheduling technique. It was a positive answer to the question of whether invention and applied research efforts could be *scheduled* by recognizing the range of uncertainty in time estimates. It made possible intelligent measurements and scheduling for creative development work.

The PERT system was in fact a communication mechanism for the brain of the Polaris organization, and became in addition a motivating factor for its mind by clearly defining the relevance and importance of each job to the success of the entire Program.

Thus, PERT provided a disciplined framework for detailed

participative planning at all levels in the Program management structure as well as for the contractors. It also provided the necessary information for identifying and seeking alternative courses of action to solve problems or exploit opportunities. Most important, it measured the predicted consequences of action on a selected alternative, in terms of time and of impact, for other efforts. It was a *complete* information system that gave essential support and focus to the decision-thinking process throughout the entire Polaris management structure.

Within the Special Projects Office, PERT was most useful in helping the Director and his staff to define key areas of responsibility and authority in the various divisions and branches of the Office. There was no strong "review and analysis" staff group (as appears in the structure of many organizations) to stand between the Director and the operating units of the Special Projects Office as a separate policing unit making performance judgments. The Navy had learned from previous experiences that most of these groups, despite original responsibilities for coordinating and synthesizing diverse activities, merely review and analyze details. The word "analyze" literally means "to break up," and that is what so often happens in the activity of review and analysis groups. They add little that is positive to program management, and destructively serve to diffuse responsibility and irritate performing units with their second-guessing inquiry.

In the Polaris Program, the operating groups themselves were given direct responsibility not only for performance in specific, assigned areas of work—such as the missile, the submarine, the navigation system, training, supply and so forth—but *also* for the integration of their work with all other work that supported or was supported by their efforts in the overall plan. Coordination of effort was an "in-line" responsibility, not something separately chartered to a detached staff group.

A Personalized Management Approach to Thinking

The personalized approach of Polaris management deserves detailed description as one of the ways in which the management developed the "mind" of the Polaris organization, and supported the decision-thinking efforts of the entire organization.

Although a great deal of performance data was computer-organized, there were named and known persons at the end of telephone lines in each organization who had identified responsibilities for some part of the entire Program. These people knew one another and dealt directly with one another throughout the entire apparatus of interacting effort. There were no anonymous "they" participants in the Program.

The Management Center and Decision-Thinking

The personalized management approach was perhaps most strongly evident in the manner in which weekly Management Center meetings were held. (The concept of a physical place called a Management Center has become widely adopted in government and industry, and such Management Center operations show up in many organizational charts.) Such centers were not posh and remote Board of Directors rooms, used infrequently and only for "top level" executive deliberations. They were rooms for meetings of the minds of the organization, designed for presentations, deliberations and decision-making by staff, as well as for senior directors who exercised their principal review function only monthly or quarterly.

In the weekly Management Center meetings, the emphasis was always on the *significance* of performance information. Each operating head reported his personal judgments as to the significance of what had happened or had failed to happen in his area of responsibility. In a disciplined format, which was time-limited in order to force careful preparation, he was required to describe the meaning of an event for his and any supporting work, as well as the action he proposed to take. The emphasis was on significance and proposed future action, rather than on explaining and giving reasons for the reported event—except as these facts directly related to proposed action. The value of these weekly meetings was far superior to that of voluminous performance reports. It was clearly recognized that the easiest way to avoid accountability was to write a one-hundred-page report on any subject and leave it to the reader to determine its significance.

The Special Projects system of accountability reporting placed its greatest emphasis on the judgment of the individual reporting as to the significance of the performance reported on. This judgment was recorded graphically for each area of his responsibility, in one of four clearly defined categories. Either work progress was in "good shape," there was a "minor weakness," there was a "major weakness," or the situation was "critical." The meaning of these terms was straightforward.

In "good shape" meant that all aspects of the Program being reported on were progressing satisfactorily, as evidenced by performance facts. There were no immediate problems which might endanger Program completion. Milestone slippages, if any, could be rescheduled without requiring a significant amount of additional effort on the part of the Special Projects Office or contractors, and without requiring rescheduling of other milestones. In other words, "Boss, don't worry, and there were a few things that happened that you might wish to compliment us about."

"Minor weakness" meant that the Program was generally progressing satisfactorily, but some event, action or delay occurred or was anticipated which would require additional effort and emphasis by the responsible operating division, the Special Projects Office and/or the contractor. No major setback was anticipated for the Program, and the resources were available with which to handle the situation. Or, "Boss, don't worry, we can fix things."

"Major weakness" meant that some event, action or delay had occurred which would impair progress toward major objectives in one or more areas, and the situation required timely action by the Director or another Branch Head. Required action might be a policy decision within the Special Projects Office, or the allocation of additional resources. In other words, "Boss, I'm in trouble and need help."

"Critical" meant that some event, action or delay had occurred which seriously impeded accomplishment of one or more major Program objectives. An appeal therefore had to be made to higher authority for a change in the Program or for additional time, money or authority to act. Or, "Boss, I think you and I are both in trouble and need help."

The weekly chart of these judgments was filed for reference. It was recognized that this approach to reporting was, in a sense, contrary to human nature. Strong and capable people do *not* like to reveal their problems before they have had a chance to solve them. For this and other reasons, many people tend to conceal their difficulties. This very human problem was solved by

1. Constant management emphasis on the <u>interdependence of</u> all Program work.
2. <u>Firm</u> management <u>discipline</u> applied to those persons who concealed their <u>difficulties</u> beyond the time they could reasonably be expected to be aware of them.
3. Generous and cooperative <u>support</u> for the effort required to solve *honestly* <u>reported</u> problems.

The fact that these personal reports and judgments were made to the Director in the presence of the reporting officer's own staff—who also attended the Management Center meeting—was a very important psychological incentive for accurate and responsible reporting. Often contractor representatives were also present.

The really *intelligent* and *critical* feature of the Polaris Program was not so much the nuts and bolts of the system like the important PERT reporting routine, but the fact that mistakes were handled in a very practical and very human way—by setting up a situation in which people could and would be the first to find and report their own failures, errors and successes.

While these weekly meetings were performance reporting occasions, they were more importantly problem identification events. The problem-solving action at these meetings was the assignment of a thinking task—including the request for a range of alternative solutions with predicted consequences—either to a line reporting group or to an ad hoc group from the Special Projects Office. Thus, the operation of the Special Projects Management Center was at the heart of the decision-thinking process in the Program.

Motivation

As a final point on the subject of personalized management, it should be reemphasized that a great deal of attention was given to the motivation of the people involved in the Polaris Program. This was done by carefully explaining and defining the objectives of the Program (answering clearly the "Why" question), and by giving generous personal and group recognitions. The purpose of this Program—which laid such heavy claim on the time, thinking ability and energy of so many people—was fully explained in film reports and briefings. This information was carried to all staff as well as to the plants and laboratories of contractors. Executives and employees, as well as their families, were included in these meetings. The films prepared as progress reports for all levels of review were also used extensively for briefings, to permit direct identification by participants with their action and thinking parts in the total Program. Credit lines and reward recognitions were given generously at all levels throughout the organization. These recognitions were given for performance that was known to be meaningful to the persons receiving them.

It is worth adding here that in standard corporate behavior much more time, money and talent are expended in public relations and the advertising of a company's identity and proud purpose to the anonymous marketplace than in communicating these same motivating messages to the company's own employees. In the Polaris management approach the "customers" were certainly told what was being done and why, but an *equal* effort was made to explain the purpose and importance of the Program to everyone who was working toward achieving its objectives.

Conclusion

The main elements of an effective deterrent force represented by a fleet ballistic missile capability as it exists today are briefly noted on the first page of this case history. Not measured in such physical terms was the impact of the Polaris management experience on the tens of thousands of men and women who, during their association with the Program in government positions or with contractors, learned that it was possible to become meaningful parts of a thinking and working organization which used their abilities at the highest level of their competence. As in any successful team effort, most of them enjoyed their individual work, and they enjoyed their accomplishments as a group.

The Director's belief in a personalized management approach was reflected in his handling of a major milestone in the Program: On July 20, 1960, in deep waters off Cape

Canaveral, Florida, the submarine USS George Washington lay ready for the *first* complete test of the Polaris weapon system. A full test firing of a submarine-launched missile was planned. Admiral Raborn did not hesitate. "Everything we know says we are ready to test this bird. Fire it!" The Polaris A-1 rose through the sea from its submarine launching chamber, ignited in midair and flew on its long course to the target area. It worked perfectly! That one successful firing by itself would have made happy headlines across the nation. Admiral Raborn wondered: "Were we just lucky that everything worked perfectly that time? I want to know." Even if a malfunction on a second firing would cancel the great news of the first shot, he did not hesitate and ordered, "Fire two!" The second shot was as successful as the first.

The thousands of men and women who had worked on this Program for over three years, from the date in early 1957 when the basic Polaris Project was first brainstormed by the Steering Task Force, were exultant. They knew their work had been successful. But they also knew that when Admiral Raborn had said "Fire two," he was also saying "Thank you," in the most meaningful way in which his appreciation and respect could be shown—with the courage of a great conviction that the team he had led had done the job that was needed.

This particular case history of the Polaris Missile Project may seem to some people far removed from normal corporate operations. It is not. It is the history of an *organization* still functioning successfully today, with over twenty years of experience. The Polaris Project dealt successfully with the problem of motivating people to a sense of purpose that extends beyond the meaning of their job descriptions; the importance of eliminating organizational and accountability barriers to thought; the need to create methods by which problems can be defined in meaningful terms; the deliberate design of means by which alternative solutions to problems can be developed and traced forward to their probable effects; and, most importantly, the open reception to ideas from all parties involved in moving proposals forward to a necessary decision—and these are all critical matters that deserve careful attention in every organization whether large or small, public or private.

There is some risk in offering this brief outline of an extremely successful management study as an illustration of the main points in this book. As we have previously noted, it is often difficult for people reading of a success story to admit that "we are not that good." It is much easier to read of a failure and say, "We are not that bad." Hopefully,

—the careful and systematic way in which questions were asked and answers sought in the Polaris Program,

—the precision with which thinking assignments were discussed and given out by the Special Projects Office and the Management Center Meetings, and

—the precise use of project assignments and project feedback, as well as the proper conduct of meetings, to overcome many of the organizational barriers to thinking which we have discussed in this book

will permit objective recognition of more familiar organizational situations, to which the basic concepts as well as some of the specific actions taken in the Polaris Program will be quite adaptable.

Systems for effective decision-thinking processes *can* be designed and made to work in all organizational environments. We believe that an understanding of the decision-thinking processes of man's mind and the mind of the organization—as well as an appreciation of the specific Polaris Program systems and procedures for carrying out thinking responsibilities—will only help to encourage the reader to improve the thinking performance of his own organization.

APPENDIX

A Suggested Format for Presenting a Proposal for Decision

The following four pages represent one of many ways in which staff work can be organized to elicit a decision on a proposed course of action.

The suggested content headings included in these representative pages would seem to be self-evident in meaning and purpose with a few possible exceptions:

1. The "Time Factor" note is included simply to indicate the desired timing of action on the proposed subject with reasons for any urgency indicated.
2. The reference to "Cognizant Personnel" is a convenient identification of specific named persons best prepared to give more detailed explanation of facts and reasoning on particular aspects of the proposal should the reader wish to have these developed further.

The introduction of this or a similar staff procedure can prove to be an effective initial probe by management of an organization's ability to handle a decision-thinking function. It can also be a good initial action leading to the deliberate development of that organizational capability.

Summarized Action Recommendation

From:
To:
Subject:

Summary of the Situation:

Basic Substance of Recommended Course of Action

Time Factor:

Principal Advantages   Possible Risks or Drawbacks

132

Statistical Supporting Data

Cognizant Personnel

Policy Comments   Operational Comments

Background Information

Pertinent Chronology

Alternative Proposals Which Were Seriously Considered

These are listed in what is considered the order of their merit. None, however, is recommended for action or serious exploration.

Principal Advantages   Possible Risks or Drawbacks

Principal Advantages   Principal Disadvantages

Principal Advantages   Possible Unfavorable Consequences

Acknowledgments

We wish to acknowledge gratefully the contributions of a number of friends and associates to the writing of this book.

Professor Edward de Bono, some of whose work and observations are cited in this book, is a serious ally of all who seek to expand and make useful an understanding of the human thinking process. His encouragement to carry this book to publication in the face of our commitments to other activity was a major influence.

Donn Tognazzini was an important monitor of our writing and of particular assistance in helping us to define and maintain a clear focus on those specific mental areas of the decision-thinking process which represent our primary concern.

We are grateful to Tom Fisher, Managing Director of the Thomas Cook Organization; David Hood, Managing Director of Unigate Dairies Ltd.; and Malcolm Wilcox, Joint Chief General Manager of the Midland Bank Group, for their friendly counsel and encouragement toward writing a book that would be short enough to prompt a first reading by a busy executive or student, but with—we trust—a useful message to which repeated reference can and will be encouraged.

We wish to thank a number of our associates who have reviewed and commented on draft manuscripts. David Bidwell, Jon Fell, John Hobson, Grahame Leman, Colin McIver and John Metcalf were most patient and perceptive friends in this requested assistance.

In specific recognition of editorial assistance, we add grateful note of the work on our manuscript by Gail Bidwell. We were most fortunate in the preparation of this book to be directly associated with the late Virginia Hilu of Harper & Row. Virginia Hilu was a professional editor in the most complete and gracious meaning of that term as it relates to the preparation of a manuscript by two neophyte authors.

Finally, we wish to thank Gracie Beiner, Anne-Marie Simonet, and Margaret Thompson for the patient and competent way in which they all worked together in the preparation, checking, and revision of the draft manuscripts involved in this jointly authored book, which required a flow of written and taped communications between two continents over a period of some four years.

While many contributed, the final product is ours, and for it we take full responsibility.

> Ben Heirs
> Gordon Pehrson

September 1976
Geneva, Switzerland
Williamsburg, Virginia